LOGAN XANDER

Mastering 3D Game Development with JavaScript: A Beginner's Guide

Harnessing the Power of JavaScript for Immersive Experiences

Contents

Introduction

3D game development has become one of the most exciting and dynamic fields in programming, offering an opportunity to create immersive, interactive worlds that captivate users. With advancements in technology, game developers now have access to tools and libraries that simplify the creation of 3D games without requiring mastery of complex languages or systems. One of the standout languages in this space is JavaScript, which has grown in popularity due to its versatility and ease of use, especially for web-based applications. In this introduction, we will explore the world of 3D game development, why JavaScript is a valuable choice for building these games, and how to set up the necessary development environment. Additionally, we'll dive into the core tools that make 3D game development with JavaScript both accessible and powerful: Three.js, Babylon.js, and WebGL.

Overview of 3D Game Development

3D game development is the process of creating video games in a three-dimensional space where objects have depth, height, and width. Unlike 2D games, which are confined to flat surfaces, 3D games offer more immersive experiences, enabling players to navigate through complex environments that simulate real-world physics and perspectives. This extra dimension provides a deeper sense of realism and interaction, making 3D games more engaging and often more challenging to develop.

Developing 3D games involves a range of elements, including:

- **3D Modeling:** Creating the assets, such as characters, environments, and objects, using specialized software like Blender or Maya.
- **Rendering:** Converting 3D models into 2D images that can be displayed on the screen, a process powered by graphics engines and libraries.
- **Physics Simulation:** Ensuring that objects in the game world behave in a realistic manner, governed by laws like gravity, collision, and inertia.
- **Lighting and Shading:** Adding lighting effects to create depth and realism, including shadows, reflections, and surface textures.
- **User Interaction:** Handling player input, such as keyboard, mouse, or game controller commands, to navigate the 3D world and manipulate objects.
- **Game Logic and AI:** Programming the rules that govern the game, including player movement, interaction with non-player characters (NPCs), and win/loss conditions.

While 3D game development can seem daunting due to the complexity of the elements involved, the advent of libraries and frameworks like Three.js and Babylon.js has significantly lowered the barrier to entry. These tools enable developers to create 3D games more easily and efficiently, even with limited experience in 3D graphics programming.

Why JavaScript for 3D Games?

JavaScript is a highly popular language, primarily known for its use in web development. However, its flexibility, performance improvements, and the rise of powerful frameworks have expanded its applications into more sophisticated domains, including 3D game development. Here are some reasons why JavaScript is a valuable choice for 3D game development: ·

1. **Web Integration:** JavaScript runs natively in web browsers, meaning developers can create 3D games that are easily accessible via the web without requiring users to download and install additional software. This makes JavaScript an ideal language for creating lightweight,

platform-independent games that can reach a broad audience.

2. **Ease of Learning:** JavaScript is known for its ease of learning and quick prototyping capabilities. Unlike languages like C++ that require a deep understanding of memory management and low-level programming, JavaScript abstracts many of these complexities, allowing developers to focus on game design and mechanics.

3. **Vast Ecosystem:** JavaScript's rich ecosystem of libraries and frameworks means that developers can leverage pre-built solutions for everything from 3D rendering (Three.js, Babylon.js) to physics simulations (Cannon.js, Ammo.js), AI (Brain.js), and more. This speeds up development and allows creators to focus on building unique game features rather than reinventing the wheel.

4. **Cross-Platform Compatibility:** JavaScript's cross-platform nature ensures that games can run on a variety of devices, including desktops, laptops, smartphones, and tablets. This is a significant advantage in a gaming market where players expect seamless experiences across multiple devices.

5. **WebGL Support:** JavaScript's integration with WebGL (Web Graphics Library) provides hardware-accelerated 3D rendering directly in the browser. This enables developers to create visually stunning games that can compete with desktop applications in terms of performance and graphical quality.

6. **Real-Time Updates:** JavaScript's asynchronous nature and real-time capabilities make it ideal for games that require dynamic updates, such as multiplayer games or games with live data feeds. JavaScript's event-driven architecture allows developers to efficiently handle multiple inputs and outputs without affecting performance.

Setting Up Your Development Environment

Before diving into 3D game development with JavaScript, it's essential to set up a suitable development environment. The process involves installing the necessary tools, libraries, and an integrated development environment (IDE) to streamline your workflow.

1. **Choose an IDE:** An Integrated Development Environment (IDE) is a critical tool for writing, testing, and debugging your code. Popular choices for JavaScript development include:

- **Visual Studio Code:** A highly popular, free, and open-source IDE that provides excellent support for JavaScript and its associated libraries. It includes features like IntelliSense, debugging tools, and extensive plugin support.
- **Sublime Text:** A lightweight, fast editor that supports multiple programming languages, including JavaScript.
- **WebStorm:** A powerful JavaScript IDE that offers intelligent coding assistance, error detection, and support for modern frameworks like Three.js and Babylon.js.

1. **Install Node.js:** Node.js is essential for setting up a JavaScript development environment, as it allows you to install and manage packages via npm (Node Package Manager). This is particularly useful when working with libraries like Three.js and Babylon.js. You can download and install Node.js from the official website (https://nodejs.org/), which will automatically include npm.
2. **Install a Local Web Server:** Since most 3D libraries rely on WebGL and require an HTTP server to serve files, setting up a local web server is recommended. This can be easily done with Node.js. Alternatively, lightweight servers like **live-server** or **http-server** can be installed globally via npm and run in your project folder.
3. **Install Libraries:** Once the environment is set up, you can install the 3D libraries needed for development:

- **Three.js:** This can be installed via npm by running npm install three in your project directory.
- **Babylon.js:** Similarly, install Babylon.js by running npm install babylonjs.

Both libraries can also be included via <script> tags in HTML for quick testing, but npm offers better management of dependencies and versioning.

1. **Set Up a Version Control System:** Using Git for version control allows you to track changes, collaborate with others, and roll back to previous versions of your game. GitHub or GitLab are excellent platforms for hosting repositories and collaborating on open-source or team-based projects.

Understanding the Core Tools: Three.js, Babylon.js, and WebGL

Several key tools power the world of 3D game development in JavaScript. Each offers unique features and advantages, making it essential to understand which tool suits your project needs.

1. **Three.js:** Three.js is a lightweight, high-level JavaScript library that simplifies the process of rendering 3D graphics in the browser using WebGL. Its abstraction over the complexities of WebGL allows developers to create intricate 3D scenes with minimal code. Key features include:

- Support for various geometric shapes and materials.
- Lighting and shading systems.
- Animation support and scene management.
- Built-in camera and controls for 3D navigation.
- Easy import of 3D models from formats like OBJ, FBX, and GLTF.

1. Three.js is especially popular for beginners and intermediate developers because of its extensive documentation and active community.
2. **Babylon.js:** Babylon.js is another powerful JavaScript framework for 3D game development, designed for creating high-performance games and applications. Babylon.js focuses on ease of use without sacrificing performance, and it integrates tightly with WebGL to provide stunning

3D visuals. Features include:

- A robust physics engine.
- Integrated animation system.
- Real-time shadow generation and rendering optimizations.
- Support for VR/AR development.
- Extensive material system, including shaders and post-processing effects.

1. Babylon.js is an excellent choice for developers aiming to create high-end, visually rich 3D games, with features like particle systems and advanced materials.
2. **WebGL:** WebGL is the foundation that enables 3D rendering in the browser. It is a low-level graphics API that allows developers to communicate directly with the GPU, providing hardware-accelerated rendering for 3D objects. While WebGL offers great flexibility and power, it requires a deep understanding of 3D graphics programming, making it more challenging to work with directly. Libraries like Three.js and Babylon.js abstract the complexities of WebGL, making it easier for developers to create games without needing to write WebGL code from scratch.

JavaScript has emerged as a powerful language for 3D game development, thanks to its accessibility, rich ecosystem, and compatibility with web technologies. With tools like Three.js, Babylon.js, and WebGL, developers can create stunning, interactive 3D games that run in the browser, reaching a global audience with ease. Setting up your development environment properly is the first step toward mastering 3D game development, and understanding the core tools will enable you to bring your creative visions to life in the virtual world. Whether you're an aspiring game developer or an experienced programmer, JavaScript offers a compelling platform for building the next generation of 3D games.

Chapter 1: Introduction to 3D Graphics

The world of 3D graphics is one of the most fascinating areas in game development. It is where artists, developers, and engineers collaborate to create immersive environments that captivate the imagination of players. In this chapter, we'll introduce some of the most fundamental concepts of 3D graphics, helping you understand how digital objects are created, manipulated, and rendered in a game world. We will start by exploring the concept of 3D rendering, the cornerstone of all visual elements in 3D games. Then, we will discuss the basics of 3D coordinate systems and how objects are positioned in a virtual space. We will also dive into key geometric structures, including vertices, edges, and faces, which form the building blocks of all 3D models. Finally, we'll look at how game engines handle 3D rendering, physics, and other elements necessary to bring a 3D game to life.

What is 3D Rendering?

At its core, **3D rendering** is the process of converting 3D models into 2D images. These images are then displayed on the screen, creating the illusion of depth and a three-dimensional space. In the simplest terms, rendering is the act of taking a 3D scene and turning it into something that can be viewed by the player. This process involves simulating how light interacts with objects, calculating the position and perspective of the camera, and finally, generating an image pixel by pixel.

The Rendering Pipeline

Rendering in modern 3D graphics involves a series of steps that are often referred to as the **rendering pipeline**. This pipeline is a sequence of processes that transform raw 3D data into the 2D images seen on the screen. The pipeline typically includes the following stages:

1. **Vertex Processing:** This is the stage where the positions of vertices (points in 3D space) are transformed into screen coordinates based on the camera's perspective. During this phase, lighting calculations are also performed.

2. **Clipping:** In this stage, objects that are outside the camera's view are removed from the rendering process to save computational resources. This step helps optimize performance by only rendering what the player can actually see.

3. **Rasterization:** Once the 3D scene is prepared, it is converted into a series of pixels in a process known as rasterization. This step converts the mathematical representation of objects into a pixel-based image.

4. **Fragment Processing:** In this stage, the color of each pixel is determined based on the material properties of the object, lighting conditions, shadows, reflections, and other effects.

5. **Output Merging:** The final image is assembled, combining the colors, textures, and effects calculated in previous stages to create the final rendered frame.

Rendering is a computationally expensive process, and performance optimization is crucial, especially in real-time applications like video games. Game engines often implement techniques such as **culling** (removing objects not visible to the camera) and **level of detail (LOD)** (adjusting the complexity of distant objects) to maintain high frame rates while rendering complex scenes.

Basics of 3D Coordinate Systems

In order to render 3D objects, it is essential to understand the concept of a **coordinate system**. A 3D coordinate system provides a way to describe the position of objects in three-dimensional space. The most common system used in 3D graphics is the **Cartesian coordinate system**, which is defined by three axes:

- **X-Axis:** Represents the horizontal direction (left-right).
- **Y-Axis:** Represents the vertical direction (up-down).
- **Z-Axis:** Represents depth (forward-backward).

These three axes intersect at a point called the **origin** (0, 0, 0), which serves as the reference point for all positions in the 3D space.

Right-Handed vs. Left-Handed Coordinate Systems

3D engines can use either a **right-handed** or a **left-handed** coordinate system, which defines the positive direction of the Z-axis.

- In a **right-handed coordinate system**, if you curl the fingers of your right hand around the Y-axis, with your thumb pointing in the positive Y direction, your fingers will point in the positive Z direction. This means that positive Z values represent depth into the scene.
- In a **left-handed coordinate system**, the positive Z direction points toward the camera. This is the system used by engines like DirectX, while OpenGL and Three.js use the right-handed system.

Knowing which coordinate system your game engine uses is important when importing models or manipulating objects, as it affects how objects are positioned and viewed in 3D space.

World, Local, and Camera Space

When working with 3D models, it's helpful to understand the different types of coordinate spaces used in rendering:

1. **World Space:** This is the global coordinate system that defines the position of objects in the entire scene relative to the world origin. Every object in the game is positioned within this world space.
2. **Local Space:** Each 3D object also has its own local coordinate system. This system defines the position of vertices and parts of the object relative to the object's origin, which may differ from the world origin. For example, a character's arm moves relative to the character's body, not the entire game world.
3. **Camera Space:** This space is relative to the camera, which means that all objects are positioned based on their relation to the camera's viewpoint. The closer an object is to the camera in Z-space, the larger it appears on the screen.

Understanding these spaces helps developers control the movement and transformation of objects in 3D games, ensuring that they behave correctly when interacting with the player, the camera, and other elements in the scene.

Understanding Vertices, Edges, and Faces

All 3D objects, from the simplest cube to the most detailed character model, are made up of basic geometric components: **vertices**, **edges**, and **faces**.

Vertices

A **vertex** is a point in 3D space, defined by its coordinates (X, Y, Z). Vertices are the most fundamental unit of a 3D model, serving as the endpoints of lines and the corners of polygons. In more complex models, vertices also hold information such as color, texture coordinates, and normal vectors (which define the direction a surface is facing).

Edges

An **edge** is a straight line that connects two vertices. Edges define the shape of a 3D object by forming the outline of polygons, which are the building blocks of the model. While edges are not rendered directly in most games, they are crucial for defining the structure of a 3D object.

Faces

A **face** is a flat surface that is enclosed by edges. In 3D modeling, faces are typically **polygons**, and the most common type of polygon used in games is the **triangle**. Triangles are favored because they are the simplest polygon and always lie flat in 3D space, making them easier to process and render. More complex shapes can be approximated by combining multiple triangles to create the illusion of smooth curves and detailed surfaces.

When multiple triangles are connected, they form a **mesh**, which is a collection of vertices, edges, and faces that together define the shape of a 3D object. The more vertices a mesh has, the more detailed it can be, but this also increases the computational cost of rendering.

How Game Engines Handle 3D

Game engines are the backbone of modern 3D game development. They provide the tools, libraries, and frameworks needed to manage rendering, physics, input handling, and other game-related tasks. A game engine abstracts many of the complexities involved in 3D rendering, allowing developers to focus on designing and building their games rather than worrying about low-level graphics programming.

Rendering with Game Engines

Most game engines, such as Unity, Unreal Engine, and Three.js, handle rendering through a combination of hardware (the GPU) and software (the engine's rendering pipeline). As we discussed earlier, rendering is a complex process that transforms 3D models into 2D images that can be displayed on the screen. Game engines optimize this process by implementing techniques such as **frustum culling** (removing objects outside the camera's view) and **back-face culling** (not rendering the backside of polygons that are not visible to the player).

Lighting and Shading

One of the most important aspects of rendering is how light interacts with objects in the scene. Game engines handle this through various lighting models that simulate how light behaves in the real world. **Shading** is the process of calculating how light affects the appearance of surfaces, and it plays a crucial role in making objects look realistic.

- **Flat shading**: Each face of an object is given a single color, making the object appear angular and faceted.
- **Smooth shading**: Colors are interpolated across a face, making the object appear smooth and rounded.
- **Phong shading**: A more advanced technique that calculates lighting per-pixel, resulting in realistic highlights and reflections.

Game engines also support advanced lighting techniques such as **global illumination**, which simulates how light bounces off surfaces and creates realistic lighting effects in the entire scene.

Physics Simulation

Game engines also manage **physics simulation**, which ensures that objects behave realistically in the game world. This includes simulating gravity, collisions, and other forces that affect the movement and interaction of objects. Many engines come with built-in physics engines (such as Unity's PhysX or Babylon.js's Cannon.js), which handle these calculations automatically.

Physics engines use mathematical models to approximate the behavior of real-world objects. For example, they might simulate how a ball bounces when it hits the ground, or how a car skids when it takes a sharp turn. Physics engines also handle **collision detection**, ensuring that objects don't pass through each other and that interactions, such as shooting or jumping, are realistic.

Chapter 2: Getting Started with Three.js

T**hree.js** is one of the most popular libraries for creating 3D graphics in JavaScript. It provides an easy-to-use interface over **WebGL**, which is a low-level graphics API built into modern browsers. By using Three.js, you can create complex 3D scenes without dealing with the intricacies of WebGL, making it a fantastic tool for developers of all skill levels. In this chapter, we will guide you through setting up Three.js, creating your first 3D scene, and understanding how to manage the render loop. By the end of this chapter, you will have a working 3D environment and a basic cube rendered on the screen.

Installing and Setting Up Three.js

Before we can start creating 3D scenes, we need to set up Three.js in our development environment. There are a few ways to include Three.js in your project, depending on whether you prefer using a CDN (Content Delivery Network), downloading the library directly, or installing it via npm (Node Package Manager).

Method 1: Using a CDN

The easiest way to get started with Three.js is by including it from a CDN. A CDN hosts the library files on a remote server, and you can link to them directly in your HTML file. This method requires no installation and is perfect for beginners.

```
html
Copy code
<!DOCTYPE html>
<html lang="en">
<head>
    <meta charset="UTF-8">
    <meta name="viewport" content="width=device-width,
    initial-scale=1.0">
    <title>Three.js Setup</title>
    <script
    src="https://cdnjs.cloudflare.com/ajax/libs/three.js/r135/three.
    min.js"></script> </head>
<body>
    <script>
        // Your Three.js code will go here
    </script>
</body>
</html>
```

Simply copy and paste the above code into an HTML file, and you're ready to go. You can now begin writing Three.js code within the <script> tag.

Method 2: Installing via npm

If you're using a build tool like **Webpack** or **Parcel**, you can install Three.js via npm. This method is preferred for more complex projects, as it allows for better dependency management and modular code.

First, initialize your project using npm:

```
bash
Copy code
npm init -y
```

Then, install Three.js:

```
bash
Copy code
```

```
npm install three
```

Once installed, you can import Three.js in your JavaScript file:

```
javascript
Copy code
import * as THREE from 'three';
```

Now that we have Three.js set up, we can move on to creating our first 3D scene.

Basic Scene Creation

Every Three.js application starts with a **scene**, a **camera**, and a **renderer**. These are the core components that make up the foundation of any 3D environment. Let's break them down:

- **Scene**: This is where all your 3D objects, lights, and cameras live. Think of it as the virtual world in which your game or application takes place.
- **Camera**: The camera defines what part of the scene is visible to the user. There are different types of cameras, but for now, we'll use the most common one: the **PerspectiveCamera**.
- **Renderer**: The renderer takes the scene and the camera and renders them into a 2D image that can be displayed on the screen.

Creating a Scene, Camera, and Renderer

Let's start by creating a basic Three.js setup that includes a scene, a camera, and a renderer. We'll also set the background color of the scene to make it more visually distinct.

```
javascript
Copy code
```

15

```javascript
// Import Three.js (skip this line if you're using a CDN)
import * as THREE from 'three';

// Create a scene
const scene = new THREE.Scene();
scene.background = new THREE.Color(0x87CEEB); // Set the
background color (light blue sky)

// Create a camera
const camera = new THREE.PerspectiveCamera(
    75, // Field of view (in degrees)
    window.innerWidth / window.innerHeight, // Aspect ratio
    0.1, // Near clipping plane
    1000 // Far clipping plane
);

// Move the camera back so we can see the objects
camera.position.z = 5;

// Create a renderer and attach it to our document
const renderer = new THREE.WebGLRenderer();
renderer.setSize(window.innerWidth, window.innerHeight); // Set
the renderer size to full window
document.body.appendChild(renderer.domElement); // Add the
renderer to the HTML document
```

In the code above:

- We create a **scene** and set its background color to light blue using scene.background = new THREE.Color(0x87CEEB).
- The **camera** is created using the **PerspectiveCamera** constructor. The camera has a field of view (FOV) of 75 degrees, and we set the aspect ratio based on the width and height of the window. The near and far clipping planes define the range of distances at which objects are visible.
- The **renderer** is responsible for displaying the scene. We set the size of the renderer to match the window's width and height, then append it to the HTML document.

At this point, you should have a blank canvas with a light blue background. Next, we'll add a simple 3D object to the scene.

Adding a Cube to the Scene

Now that we have a scene, camera, and renderer, it's time to add a basic 3D object—a **cube**. In Three.js, objects are created using **geometries** and **materials**.

- **Geometries** define the shape of an object (e.g., a cube, sphere, plane).
- **Materials** define how the surface of an object looks (e.g., color, texture, reflectivity).

Let's create a cube using the BoxGeometry class and give it a simple material.

```javascript
Copy code
// Create a cube geometry (width, height, depth)
const geometry = new THREE.BoxGeometry(1, 1, 1);

// Create a basic material and set its color
const material = new THREE.MeshBasicMaterial({ color: 0x00ff00 });

// Create a mesh by combining the geometry and material
const cube = new THREE.Mesh(geometry, material);

// Add the cube to the scene
scene.add(cube);
```

In this code, we:

- Create a BoxGeometry with dimensions 1x1x1 (a cube).
- Create a MeshBasicMaterial and set its color to green (0x00ff00).
- Combine the geometry and material to create a **mesh**. A mesh is the visible 3D object that is rendered in the scene.
- Add the cube to the scene using scene.add(cube).

At this point, you should have a green cube in the middle of your screen, but we can't see it yet because we haven't rendered the scene. That's where the render loop comes in.

Working with the Render Loop

Rendering a 3D scene in a game or interactive application requires a continuous update loop. This loop constantly renders the scene at a set frame rate, giving the illusion of smooth motion. In Three.js, this loop is often referred to as the **render loop** or **animation loop**.

The Basic Render Loop

To create a render loop, we define a function that repeatedly renders the scene and updates any animations or changes in the scene. We use the requestAnimationFrame function to ensure that the loop runs efficiently and adapts to the display's refresh rate.

```javascript
Copy code
function animate() {
    requestAnimationFrame(animate);

    // Optional: Rotate the cube for demonstration purposes
    cube.rotation.x += 0.01;
    cube.rotation.y += 0.01;

    // Render the scene from the perspective of the camera
    renderer.render(scene, camera);
}

// Start the animation loop
animate();
```

In this code:

- We define the animate function, which will be called repeatedly to update the scene.
- Inside the function, we rotate the cube slightly on the X and Y axes using

```javascript
Copy code
const boxGeometry = new THREE.BoxGeometry(1, 1, 1); // Width,
height, and depth
const boxMaterial = new THREE.MeshBasicMaterial({ color: 0x00ff00
});
const boxMesh = new THREE.Mesh(boxGeometry, boxMaterial);
scene.add(boxMesh);
```

In the example above, we create a cube with dimensions 1x1x1 and apply a green material to it. The BoxGeometry constructor takes width, height, and depth as parameters. Once created, the cube is added to the scene using scene.add().

Sphere Geometry

A **sphere geometry** is another essential shape in 3D games. It's useful for objects like planets, balls, or any round shapes. The SphereGeometry class lets you easily create spheres with a specified radius and number of segments.

```javascript
Copy code
const sphereGeometry = new THREE.SphereGeometry(1, 32, 32); //
Radius, width segments, height segments
const sphereMaterial = new THREE.MeshBasicMaterial({ color:
0xff0000 });
const sphereMesh = new THREE.Mesh(sphereGeometry, sphereMaterial);
scene.add(sphereMesh);
```

Here, we create a sphere with a radius of 1 and 32 segments along the width and height. The more segments, the smoother the sphere will appear. The material is set to red, and the sphere is added to the scene.

Other Basic Geometries

Three.js offers a variety of other built-in geometries that can be used to create different shapes:

- **CylinderGeometry**: For creating cylinders or cones.

- **PlaneGeometry**: For flat surfaces like floors or walls.
- **TorusGeometry**: For donut-like shapes (useful for rings or tires).
- **IcosahedronGeometry**: For more complex, polyhedral shapes.

For example, to create a torus (donut shape):

```javascript
Copy code
const torusGeometry = new THREE.TorusGeometry(1, 0.4, 16, 100); //
Radius, tube radius, radial segments, tubular segments
const torusMaterial = new THREE.MeshBasicMaterial({ color:
0x0000ff });
const torusMesh = new THREE.Mesh(torusGeometry, torusMaterial);
scene.add(torusMesh);
```

Applying Materials: MeshBasicMaterial, MeshPhongMaterial

In Three.js, materials control the appearance of 3D objects. They define how the surface of a geometry looks, including its color, reflectivity, and interaction with light. Different types of materials are available, each with unique properties.

MeshBasicMaterial

MeshBasicMaterial is the most basic type of material. It defines a solid color or texture for an object but does not interact with lights in the scene. This material is ideal for simple objects where lighting effects are unnecessary.

```javascript
Copy code
const basicMaterial = new THREE.MeshBasicMaterial({ color:
0x00ff00 });
const cube = new THREE.Mesh(new THREE.BoxGeometry(1, 1, 1),
basicMaterial);
scene.add(cube);
```

MeshBasicMaterial is great for objects that don't need to respond to light sources, such as user interface elements or backgrounds.

MeshPhongMaterial

For more realistic materials that react to light, you can use MeshPhongMaterial. This material supports specular highlights (shiny spots) and shading based on the lighting in the scene, giving objects a more three-dimensional look.

```javascript
Copy code
const phongMaterial = new THREE.MeshPhongMaterial({
    color: 0x2194ce, // Base color
    specular: 0x111111, // Color of the shiny highlights
    shininess: 30, // Intensity of the shiny effect
});
const sphere = new THREE.Mesh(new THREE.SphereGeometry(1, 32, 32),
phongMaterial);
scene.add(sphere);
```

In this example, we create a sphere with a MeshPhongMaterial. The material's specular property defines the color of the shiny highlights, and the shininess property controls how shiny the material appears. Objects with MeshPhongMaterial reflect light in a realistic way, making them suitable for metallic or glossy surfaces.

Working with Textures and UV Mapping

Textures are images that can be applied to the surface of a 3D object to give it more detail, such as wood grain, metal, or grass. Applying textures in Three.js is straightforward, and it involves using the TextureLoader class to load an image and then assigning it to a material.

Applying a Texture to a Cube

```javascript
Copy code
```

```
const textureLoader = new THREE.TextureLoader();
const texture = textureLoader.load('path/to/texture.jpg');
const texturedMaterial = new THREE.MeshBasicMaterial({ map:
texture });
const texturedCube = new THREE.Mesh(new THREE.BoxGeometry(1, 1,
1), texturedMaterial);
scene.add(texturedCube);
```

In this code, we use TextureLoader to load an image from a file and then assign it to the map property of MeshBasicMaterial. The texture is applied to the surface of the cube, giving it a more detailed appearance.

UV Mapping

When applying a texture to a 3D object, the texture must be mapped correctly onto the object's surface. This process is called **UV mapping**. The "U" and "V" refer to the axes of the 2D texture image, while "X", "Y", and "Z" are the axes of the 3D geometry.

Three.js automatically handles UV mapping for most built-in geometries, but if you create custom geometries or complex shapes, you may need to manually define how textures are mapped to the surface. You can modify UV mapping by manipulating the geometry's uv attribute, though for beginners, the built-in UV mapping is typically sufficient.

Controlling Light and Shadows in the Scene

Lighting is an essential part of 3D game development, as it adds depth and realism to your scenes. In Three.js, different types of lights can be added to a scene, and objects can cast and receive shadows for enhanced realism.

Types of Lights in Three.js

Three.js offers several types of lights that can be used to illuminate your scene:

1. **Ambient Light**: Provides global, non-directional light that affects all objects equally. It is useful for adding a base level of brightness to the scene.

```javascript
Copy code
const ambientLight = new THREE.AmbientLight(0xffffff, 0.5); //
Color, intensity
scene.add(ambientLight);
```

1. **Directional Light**: Acts like sunlight, casting light in a specific direction. It can cast shadows and is ideal for outdoor environments.

```javascript
Copy code
const directionalLight = new THREE.DirectionalLight(0xffffff, 1);
directionalLight.position.set(5, 10, 7.5);
scene.add(directionalLight);
```

1. **Point Light**: Emits light from a single point, radiating outward in all directions, similar to a lightbulb.

```javascript
Copy code
const pointLight = new THREE.PointLight(0xffffff, 1, 100); //
Color, intensity, distance
pointLight.position.set(5, 5, 5);
scene.add(pointLight);
```

1. **SpotLight**: Emits light in a cone shape, similar to a flashlight or a spotlight.

```javascript
Copy code
const spotLight = new THREE.SpotLight(0xffffff);
spotLight.position.set(10, 20, 10);
scene.add(spotLight);
```

Enabling Shadows

To add realism to your scene, you can enable shadows in Three.js. Shadows are not enabled by default, so you need to activate them on both the light source and the objects that cast and receive shadows.

1. **Enable shadows on the renderer**:

```javascript
Copy code
renderer.shadowMap.enabled = true;
```

1. **Enable shadows on the light**:

```javascript
Copy code
const light = new THREE.DirectionalLight(0xffffff, 1);
light.castShadow = true;
scene.add(light);
```

1. **Enable shadows on objects**:

```javascript
Copy code
const cube = new THREE.Mesh(boxGeometry, boxMaterial);
cube.castShadow = true; // Object casts shadows
cube.receiveShadow = true; // Object receives shadows
scene.add(cube);
```

Shadows add a great deal of realism to 3D scenes, especially in games where lighting can change dynamically. Experimenting with light intensity.

While we've covered the basic aspects of geometry and materials, there are additional considerations and techniques that can further enhance your 3D scenes. This section will delve deeper into advanced geometries, more complex materials, and techniques for optimizing your 3D assets.

Advanced Geometries

In addition to the basic geometries provided by Three.js, you can create more complex shapes using custom geometries or by modifying existing ones.

Custom Geometries

You can define custom geometries using the BufferGeometry class, which provides more flexibility and efficiency. This class allows you to define your own vertices, normals, and UVs, which is particularly useful for more intricate models or when performance is critical.

```javascript
Copy code
const vertices = new Float32Array([
    // X, Y, Z coordinates
    -1, -1, 0,
     1, -1, 0,
     0,  1, 0,
]);

const customGeometry = new THREE.BufferGeometry();
customGeometry.setAttribute('position', new
```

```
THREE.BufferAttribute(vertices, 3));
const customMaterial = new THREE.MeshBasicMaterial({ color:
0xffff00 });
const customMesh = new THREE.Mesh(customGeometry, customMaterial);
scene.add(customMesh);
```

In this example, we create a simple triangle using BufferGeometry. You can add more attributes like colors, normals, and UVs for more complex models.

Geometry Modifiers

Three.js also provides modifiers like THREE.SphereBufferGeometry or THREE.CylinderBufferGeometry, which can be used to create variations of basic geometries by adjusting parameters like radius, height, and segments. You can combine these shapes to create unique objects, like using the THREE.Group class to group several geometries together.

```
javascript
Copy code
const group = new THREE.Group();
const cylinder = new THREE.Mesh(new THREE.CylinderGeometry(0.5,
0.5, 2, 32), new THREE.MeshPhongMaterial({ color: 0x888888 }));
const box = new THREE.Mesh(new THREE.BoxGeometry(1, 1, 1), new
THREE.MeshPhongMaterial({ color: 0x00ff00 }));
box.position.y = 1; // Raise the box above the cylinder
group.add(cylinder);
group.add(box);
scene.add(group);
```

Enhanced Material Options

Beyond MeshBasicMaterial and MeshPhongMaterial, Three.js offers a range of other materials that provide advanced features.

MeshStandardMaterial

MeshStandardMaterial is a physically based material that simulates real-world properties of materials more accurately. It requires a light source and works well for achieving realistic rendering.

```javascript
Copy code
const standardMaterial = new THREE.MeshStandardMaterial({
    color: 0x00ff00,
    roughness: 0.5, // Control how rough or smooth the surface is
    metalness: 0.5, // Control the metallic properties of the
    surface
});
const standardCube = new THREE.Mesh(new THREE.BoxGeometry(1, 1,
1), standardMaterial);
scene.add(standardCube);
```

MeshPhysicalMaterial

For even more realism, MeshPhysicalMaterial builds on MeshStandard-Material and adds additional properties like clear coat and transmission for simulating transparent or shiny surfaces.

```javascript
Copy code
const physicalMaterial = new THREE.MeshPhysicalMaterial({
    color: 0x2194ce,
    clearcoat: 1.0, // How shiny the surface is
    clearcoatRoughness: 0.1, // Roughness of the clear coat
});
const physicalSphere = new THREE.Mesh(new THREE.SphereGeometry(1,
32, 32), physicalMaterial);
scene.add(physicalSphere);
```

Texture Mapping Techniques

Beyond basic texture application, understanding different mapping techniques can enhance how textures interact with your models.

Normal Mapping

Normal mapping simulates the appearance of small surface details without adding extra geometry. By using a normal map, you can create the illusion of depth and detail on a flat surface.

```javascript
Copy code
const textureLoader = new THREE.TextureLoader();
const normalMap = textureLoader.load('path/to/normalMap.jpg');
const normalMaterial = new THREE.MeshStandardMaterial({
    map: texture,
    normalMap: normalMap,
});
const normalMappedCube = new THREE.Mesh(new THREE.BoxGeometry(1,
1, 1), normalMaterial);
scene.add(normalMappedCube);
```

Bump Mapping

Bump mapping is similar to normal mapping but provides a less detailed effect. It uses a grayscale image to affect the surface normals of the material.

```javascript
Copy code
const bumpMap = textureLoader.load('path/to/bumpMap.jpg');
const bumpMaterial = new THREE.MeshStandardMaterial({
    map: texture,
    bumpMap: bumpMap,
    bumpScale: 0.1, // Scale of the bump effect
});
const bumpMappedSphere = new THREE.Mesh(new
THREE.SphereGeometry(1, 32, 32), bumpMaterial);
scene.add(bumpMappedSphere);
```

Optimizing 3D Assets

As you build more complex scenes, performance can become an issue, especially for web-based applications. Here are some optimization techniques:

Reduce Polygon Count

Using simpler geometries can significantly improve performance. Consider reducing the polygon count for distant objects or using LOD (Level of Detail) techniques, where simpler models are used at a distance.

Texture Atlases

Instead of using multiple small textures, create a texture atlas—an image that contains several smaller images. This reduces the number of texture switches in your rendering loop, improving performance.

Instancing

If you have many identical objects in your scene (like trees or rocks), use instancing. Three.js provides instancing support through the InstancedMesh class, which allows you to render multiple copies of the same geometry with less overhead.

```javascript
Copy code
const count = 100; // Number of instances
const instancedMesh = new THREE.InstancedMesh(boxGeometry,
boxMaterial, count);

for (let i = 0; i < count; i++) {
    const matrix = new THREE.Matrix4();
    matrix.setPosition(Math.random() * 10, 0, Math.random() * 10);
    // Random positions
    instancedMesh.setMatrixAt(i, matrix);
}
scene.add(instancedMesh);
```

In this chapter, we've explored the intricacies of geometry and materials in Three.js, focusing on how to create various shapes, apply materials, and enhance your 3D scenes with textures and lighting. Understanding these concepts is crucial for building engaging and visually appealing 3D games. As you progress in your development journey, continue experimenting with different geometries, materials, and optimization techniques to find your unique artistic style and approach to game development.

In the next chapter, we will discuss animation techniques to bring your 3D models to life, including keyframe animations, bone animations, and how to work with animation libraries in Three.js. This knowledge will allow you to create more dynamic and interactive experiences in your games.

Chapter 4: Camera, Lights, and Action

I n the world of 3D game development, the visual experience is crafted not only through models and textures but also through the careful arrangement of cameras and lighting. In this chapter, we will explore how to effectively utilize cameras and lighting to enhance the mood and perception of your 3D environment. By mastering these elements, you will gain the ability to create immersive experiences that captivate players. We will cover the following topics:

1. **Types of Cameras: Perspective vs. Orthographic**
2. **Configuring and Moving the Camera**
3. **Adding Lights: Directional, Point, Ambient, and Spotlights**
4. **Creating Dynamic Shadows and Reflections**

Types of Cameras: Perspective vs. Orthographic

In Three.js, you have the option of using different camera types to control how the scene is viewed. The two primary types are perspective cameras and orthographic cameras.

Perspective Camera

A perspective camera simulates the way human eyes perceive the world. Objects closer to the camera appear larger, while objects further away appear smaller, creating a sense of depth. This is achieved through a field of view

(FOV) parameter that determines the angle of view.

Creating a Perspective Camera

To create a perspective camera in Three.js, you can use the THREE.Perspe ctiveCamera class. Here's an example of how to set one up:

```javascript
Copy code
const fieldOfView = 75; // Degrees
const aspectRatio = window.innerWidth / window.innerHeight; //
Aspect ratio
const nearClippingPlane = 0.1; // Near clipping plane
const farClippingPlane = 1000; // Far clipping plane

const camera = new THREE.PerspectiveCamera(fieldOfView,
aspectRatio, nearClippingPlane, farClippingPlane);
camera.position.set(0, 1, 5); // Set the initial position of the
camera
```

The fieldOfView parameter is measured in degrees, and a typical value is around 75 degrees. The aspectRatio is calculated based on the width and height of the window to ensure that the aspect ratio of the rendered scene matches the viewport. The nearClippingPlane and farClippingPlane define the distances from the camera at which objects are rendered.

Orthographic Camera

An orthographic camera provides a different visual perspective where objects maintain their size regardless of their distance from the camera. This means that parallel lines remain parallel, making it suitable for 2D games or certain 3D applications where depth perception is not a priority.

Creating an Orthographic Camera

To create an orthographic camera in Three.js, use the THREE.Orthographi cCamera class. Here's how you can set one up:

```javascript
Copy code
const frustumSize = 10; // Size of the view frustum
const orthographicCamera = new THREE.OrthographicCamera(
    frustumSize / -2, // Left
    frustumSize / 2,  // Right
    frustumSize / 2,  // Top
    frustumSize / -2, // Bottom
    nearClippingPlane,
    farClippingPlane
);

orthographicCamera.position.set(0, 5, 10); // Set the camera
position
orthographicCamera.lookAt(0, 0, 0); // Look at the center of the
scene
```

In this example, the frustumSize determines the size of the viewable area. The parameters for the orthographic camera define the left, right, top, and bottom bounds of the frustum, along with the near and far clipping planes.

Choosing Between Perspective and Orthographic

When deciding between perspective and orthographic cameras, consider the visual style and gameplay mechanics of your project. Perspective cameras are ideal for 3D environments that require depth perception, while orthographic cameras work well for 2D or isometric games.

Configuring and Moving the Camera

Once you've chosen the type of camera, the next step is to configure it and implement movement. In most games, the camera should follow the player or adapt to the environment dynamically.

Configuring the Camera

You can configure various properties of the camera, such as its position, rotation, and field of view, to create the desired visual effect. To allow for smooth transitions and camera control, you can also use libraries such as dat.GUI for creating user interfaces that modify camera properties in real-time.

Example of Configuring the Camera

Here's how to configure a perspective camera:

```javascript
Copy code
function configureCamera() {
    camera.position.set(0, 1, 5); // Set initial position
    camera.lookAt(0, 0, 0); // Look at the scene's center
}

// Call the function to configure the camera
configureCamera();
```

Moving the Camera

There are various ways to move the camera in a 3D environment:

1. **Static Camera**: The camera remains fixed at a specific position. This approach is common in platformers or puzzle games where the action occurs in a defined area.
2. **Following Camera**: The camera tracks a player or object as it moves through the scene. This is commonly used in third-person and first-person games.
3. **Free-Form Camera**: The camera can move freely around the scene, allowing for a more dynamic perspective. This type of camera can be controlled using mouse movements or keyboard inputs.

Example of a Following Camera

Here's a simple implementation of a following camera that tracks a moving object:

```javascript
Copy code
function updateCameraPosition(targetObject) {
    camera.position.x = targetObject.position.x;
    camera.position.y = targetObject.position.y + 1; // Slightly
    above the object
    camera.position.z = targetObject.position.z + 5; // Behind the
    object
    camera.lookAt(targetObject.position); // Look at the object
}

// In your animation loop
function animate() {
    requestAnimationFrame(animate);
    updateCameraPosition(player); // Assuming 'player' is your
    target object
    renderer.render(scene, camera);
}
```

In this example, the camera's position is updated each frame based on the target object's position, ensuring a smooth following effect.

Adding Lights: Directional, Point, Ambient, and Spotlights

Lighting is crucial in 3D environments as it affects the mood and visibility of the scene. In Three.js, you can add various types of lights to create realistic or stylized effects.

Directional Light

Directional lights simulate sunlight or other distant light sources. They cast parallel light rays, making them ideal for outdoor scenes. To create a directional light:

```javascript
Copy code
const directionalLight = new THREE.DirectionalLight(0xffffff, 1);
// Color and intensity
directionalLight.position.set(5, 10, 7); // Position the light
scene.add(directionalLight);
```

You can also adjust the castShadow property to create shadows:

```javascript
Copy code
directionalLight.castShadow = true;
```

Point Light

Point lights emit light in all directions from a single point, similar to a light bulb. They can create localized lighting effects and are suitable for indoor scenes.

```javascript
Copy code
const pointLight = new THREE.PointLight(0xffffff, 1, 100); //
Color, intensity, and distance
pointLight.position.set(0, 10, 0); // Position the light
scene.add(pointLight);
```

Ambient Light

Ambient light provides a base level of illumination in the scene without a specific direction. It helps prevent harsh shadows and creates a more evenly lit environment.

```javascript
Copy code
const ambientLight = new THREE.AmbientLight(0x404040); // Soft
white color
scene.add(ambientLight);
```

Spotlight

Spotlights project light in a specific direction, creating a cone of light. They are useful for simulating effects like headlights or theatrical lighting.

```javascript
Copy code
const spotLight = new THREE.SpotLight(0xffffff);
spotLight.position.set(0, 10, 0);
spotLight.angle = Math.PI / 6; // Cone angle
spotLight.penumbra = 0.1; // Softness of the edges
scene.add(spotLight);
```

Combining Lights

In many cases, a combination of lights can create a more immersive atmosphere. You might use ambient light for base illumination, directional light for shadows, and point lights for highlights or effects.

Light Helpers

Three.js provides helpers for visualizing light sources in the scene, which can be invaluable during development.

```javascript
Copy code
const directionalLightHelper = new
THREE.DirectionalLightHelper(directionalLight, 5);
scene.add(directionalLightHelper);
```

This will display a visual representation of the directional light's direction and intensity.

Creating Dynamic Shadows and Reflections

Shadows and reflections add depth and realism to 3D environments. In Three.js, creating dynamic shadows and reflections requires careful setup of lights, materials, and renderers.

Creating Shadows

To enable shadows in Three.js, you need to configure both the light source and the objects that will cast and receive shadows.

Enabling Shadows on Lights

First, enable shadows for the light source:

```javascript
Copy code
directionalLight.castShadow = true; // For directional light
```

Enabling Shadows on Objects

Next, set the objects to cast and receive shadows:

```javascript
Copy code
const boxGeometry = new THREE.BoxGeometry(1, 1, 1);
const boxMaterial = new THREE.MeshStandardMaterial({ color:
```

```
0x00ff00 });

const box = new THREE.Mesh(boxGeometry, boxMaterial);
box.castShadow = true; // Cast shadows
box.receiveShadow = true; // Receive shadows
scene.add(box);
```

Configuring Shadow Properties

You can configure shadow properties on the light source for better visual effects:

```javascript
Copy code
directionalLight.shadow.mapSize.width = 1024; // Size of the
shadow map
directionalLight.shadow.mapSize.height = 1024;
directionalLight.shadow.camera.near = 0.5; // Near clipping plane
for shadows
directionalLight.shadow.camera.far = 50; // Far clipping plane for
shadows
```

Creating Reflections

Creating realistic reflections can enhance the visual fidelity of your scene. Three.js offers several techniques for reflections, including cube maps and reflective materials.

Using Cube Maps for Reflections

Cube maps are useful for simulating reflective surfaces like water or shiny objects. To create a cube map, you need six images representing the environment in each direction.

```javascript
Copy code
const cubeTextureLoader = new THREE.CubeTextureLoader();
const texture = cubeTextureLoader.load([
    'path/to/posx.jpg', 'path/to/negx.jpg',
    'path/to/posy.jpg', 'path/to/negy.jpg',
    'path/to/posz.jpg', 'path/to/negz.jpg',
]);

scene.background = texture; // Set the scene's background to the
cube map
```

Using Reflective Materials

You can also use reflective materials such as THREE.MeshStandardMaterial or THREE.MeshPhongMaterial with an environment map to create reflections.

```javascript
Copy code
const reflectiveMaterial = new THREE.MeshStandardMaterial({
    color: 0xffffff,
    envMap: texture, // The environment map for reflections
    metalness: 1, // Adjust for a more metallic appearance
    roughness: 0.1 // Adjust for a smooth surface
});

const reflectiveBox = new THREE.Mesh(boxGeometry,
reflectiveMaterial);
scene.add(reflectiveBox);
```

In this chapter, we explored the fundamental elements of camera control and lighting in Three.js. By understanding the different types of cameras and their configurations, you can create dynamic perspectives that enhance the player's experience. Additionally, with various types of lights at your disposal, you can set the mood of your scene and provide necessary illumination.

Finally, by implementing shadows and reflections, you add depth and realism to your 3D environments. With these techniques, you are now better equipped to create visually stunning and immersive games using JavaScript and Three.js. As we move forward in the book, we will continue to build on these concepts and apply them to more complex scenes and interactions.

Chapter 5: Building Interactive Elements

In the realm of 3D game development, interactivity is crucial for engaging players and creating immersive experiences. This chapter will delve into the key aspects of building interactive elements in your 3D game using Three.js. We will cover handling user input through mouse and keyboard controls, adding clickable objects, creating basic animations, and introducing the concept of physics, particularly focusing on basic collision detection.

Handling User Input: Mouse and Keyboard Controls

Interactivity begins with user input. In a 3D environment, users typically interact through mouse and keyboard controls. Three.js provides an easy way to capture and respond to these inputs, allowing you to create responsive and engaging gameplay.

Mouse Controls

You can capture mouse movements and clicks using the MouseEvent object. To track the mouse position, you need to update a global variable whenever the mouse moves. You can then use this position to interact with objects in your scene.

```javascript
Copy code
let mouse = new THREE.Vector2();
let raycaster = new THREE.Raycaster();
```

```
function onMouseMove(event) {
    // Convert the mouse position to normalized device coordinates
    mouse.x = (event.clientX / window.innerWidth) * 2 - 1;
    mouse.y = -(event.clientY / window.innerHeight) * 2 + 1;
}

window.addEventListener('mousemove', onMouseMove, false);
```

With the mouse position captured, you can use Raycaster to detect which objects are intersected by the mouse ray. This is essential for implementing clickable objects.

Keyboard Controls

To capture keyboard input, you can listen for keydown and keyup events. This allows you to perform actions based on specific key presses.

```
javascript
Copy code
let keys = {};

function onKeyDown(event) {
    keys[event.code] = true; // Mark the key as pressed
}

function onKeyUp(event) {
    keys[event.code] = false; // Mark the key as released
}

window.addEventListener('keydown', onKeyDown, false);
window.addEventListener('keyup', onKeyUp, false);
```

In your animation loop, you can check the state of keys to perform actions like moving an object or triggering animations.

```
javascript
Copy code
function animate() {
    requestAnimationFrame(animate);
```

```
    // Move an object based on keyboard input
    if (keys['ArrowUp']) {
        object.position.z -= 0.1; // Move forward
    }
    if (keys['ArrowDown']) {
        object.position.z += 0.1; // Move backward
    }

    renderer.render(scene, camera);
}
animate();
```

Adding Clickable Objects

With the input handling set up, the next step is to create clickable objects. This adds a layer of interactivity, allowing players to engage with your game world meaningfully.

Creating Clickable Objects

To create clickable objects, you can use the Raycaster we discussed earlier. When a user clicks on the canvas, you can check if the click intersects any objects in your scene.

```javascript
Copy code
function onClick(event) {
    // Update the mouse variable with the click position
    mouse.x = (event.clientX / window.innerWidth) * 2 - 1;
    mouse.y = -(event.clientY / window.innerHeight) * 2 + 1;

    // Calculate objects intersecting the picking ray
    raycaster.setFromCamera(mouse, camera);
    const intersects = raycaster.intersectObjects(scene.children);

    if (intersects.length > 0) {
        const clickedObject = intersects[0].object;
```

```
        // Perform action on the clicked object
        clickedObject.material.color.set(0xff0000); // Change
        color as an example
    }
}

window.addEventListener('click', onClick, false);
```

This code sets up a click event listener that detects which object was clicked and performs an action—changing the object's color in this case. You can extend this functionality to trigger animations, display messages, or interact with other game elements.

Creating Basic Animations

Animating objects in your 3D scene adds life and dynamism, enhancing user engagement. In this section, we'll cover how to create basic animations using Three.js.

Simple Transformations

You can animate objects by modifying their properties over time, such as position, rotation, and scale. Here's an example of animating a cube to rotate continuously:

```javascript
Copy code
function animate() {
    requestAnimationFrame(animate);

    // Rotate the cube
    cube.rotation.x += 0.01;
    cube.rotation.y += 0.01;

    renderer.render(scene, camera);
}
animate();
```

This creates a simple animation where the cube rotates around its axes. You can enhance the animation by varying the rotation speed or applying easing functions for smoother transitions.

Tweening Libraries

For more complex animations, consider using tweening libraries like GSAP (GreenSock Animation Platform). These libraries provide powerful tools for animating properties with easing, delays, and more.

To use GSAP, you first need to install it via npm or include it in your HTML:

```html
html
Copy code
<script
src="https://cdnjs.cloudflare.com/ajax/libs/gsap/3.6.0/gsap.min.js"></script>
```

You can then create animations like this:

```javascript
javascript
Copy code
gsap.to(cube.rotation, {
    duration: 2,
    x: Math.PI * 2, // Rotate 360 degrees
    onComplete: () => {
        // Action to take when the animation is complete
        console.log('Rotation complete!');
    },
});
```

GSAP simplifies the process of creating smooth and visually appealing animations, making it a popular choice among developers.

Introduction to Physics: Basic Collision Detection

Physics is an essential component of interactive 3D games. Understanding how to implement basic collision detection can enhance gameplay and make interactions feel more realistic.

Basic Collision Detection

In Three.js, you can perform simple collision detection using bounding boxes or spheres. Every object in your scene has a bounding box that can be used to check for intersections with other objects.

```javascript
Copy code
// Check for collision between two objects
function checkCollision(objectA, objectB) {
    objectA.geometry.computeBoundingBox();
    objectB.geometry.computeBoundingBox();

    const boxA = objectA.geometry.boundingBox.clone();
    const boxB = objectB.geometry.boundingBox.clone();

    boxA.applyMatrix4(objectA.matrixWorld);
    boxB.applyMatrix4(objectB.matrixWorld);

    return boxA.intersectsBox(boxB);
}

// Usage example
if (checkCollision(cube, otherObject)) {
    console.log('Collision detected!');
}
```

In this example, we compute the bounding boxes of two objects and check if they intersect. If they do, you can respond accordingly, such as triggering an animation, sound effect, or game event.

Physics Engines

For more complex physics interactions, consider integrating a physics engine like Cannon.js or Ammo.js. These libraries provide robust physics simulations, including rigid body dynamics, gravity, and collision responses.

Here's a brief overview of how to set up Cannon.js for collision detection:

1. **Install Cannon.js**: You can add Cannon.js to your project via npm or include it in your HTML.

```html
html
Copy code
<script
src="https://cdn.rawgit.com/schteppe/cannon.js/master/build/cannon
.min.js"></script>
```

1. **Create a World**: Set up a physics world where you can add bodies and constraints.

```javascript
javascript
Copy code
const world = new CANNON.World();
world.gravity.set(0, -9.82, 0); // Set gravity

// Create a box body
const boxShape = new CANNON.Box(new CANNON.Vec3(1, 1, 1));
const boxBody = new CANNON.Body({
    mass: 1,
});
boxBody.addShape(boxShape);
world.addBody(boxBody);
```

1. **Step the Simulation**: In your animation loop, step the physics world to update the positions of your bodies.

```javascript
javascript
Copy code
function animate() {
    requestAnimationFrame(animate);
    world.step(1 / 60); // Step the physics world
    // Update Three.js mesh positions based on physics bodies
```

```
    cube.position.copy(boxBody.position);
    cube.quaternion.copy(boxBody.quaternion);
    renderer.render(scene, camera);
  }
  animate();
```

Integrating a physics engine allows you to create more realistic interactions, such as bouncing, rolling, and sliding.

In this chapter, we have covered the essential components of building interactive elements in your Three.js 3D game. By handling user input through mouse and keyboard controls, adding clickable objects, creating basic animations, and introducing physics concepts, you can enhance the interactivity and engagement of your game.

As you continue developing your 3D projects, experiment with these techniques to create a richer, more immersive experience for your players. In the next chapter, we will explore advanced animation techniques, such as skeletal animations and morph targets, to further elevate your game development skills.

Chapter 6: Working with 3D Models

In 3D game development, the visual richness of your environment heavily relies on the models you incorporate. This chapter will explore how to import 3D models into your game using Three.js, animate these models, and optimize them for performance. By the end of this chapter, you'll be equipped to enhance your game with beautifully crafted 3D assets.

Importing 3D Models into Your Game

Before you can use 3D models in your game, you need to understand the various formats available and how to effectively load them into Three.js.

Formats: OBJ, FBX, GLTF

There are several common file formats for 3D models, each with its own characteristics and use cases:

- **OBJ**: The OBJ format is one of the oldest and simplest formats for 3D models. It supports geometry and UV mapping but does not include animations or complex materials. OBJ files are great for static models but are limited in terms of advanced features.
- **FBX**: The FBX (Filmbox) format is widely used in the industry for its ability to store complex models, animations, and rigging information. It is particularly popular among game developers and animation studios. FBX files can be large and may require additional tools for conversion, but they offer great flexibility.
- **GLTF**: The GLTF (GL Transmission Format) is becoming the standard

for transmitting 3D models on the web. It supports advanced features such as animations, materials, and textures, all while being optimized for efficient loading. GLTF files are often referred to as the "JPEG of 3D" due to their compact size and ease of use.

Loading Models in Three.js

Three.js provides loaders for each of these formats, making it straightforward to incorporate models into your game. Below, we'll cover how to load models using Three.js loaders.

Loading an OBJ Model

To load an OBJ model, you need the OBJLoader class. Ensure you include the loader script in your project.

```html
Copy code
<script
src="https://threejs.org/examples/js/loaders/OBJLoader.js"></script>
```

Here's an example of loading an OBJ model:

```javascript
Copy code
const loader = new THREE.OBJLoader();
loader.load('path/to/model.obj', (object) => {
    scene.add(object);
});
```

Loading an FBX Model

To load an FBX model, you will need the FBXLoader class:

```html
Copy code
<script
src="https://threejs.org/examples/js/loaders/FBXLoader.js"></script>
```

Loading an FBX model looks like this:

```javascript
Copy code
const fbxLoader = new THREE.FBXLoader();
fbxLoader.load('path/to/model.fbx', (object) => {
    scene.add(object);
});
```

Loading a GLTF Model

Loading a GLTF model is done with the GLTFLoader. Make sure to include the following script:

```html
Copy code
<script
src="https://threejs.org/examples/js/loaders/GLTFLoader.js"></script>
```

Here's how to load a GLTF model:

```javascript
Copy code
const gltfLoader = new THREE.GLTFLoader();
gltfLoader.load('path/to/model.gltf', (gltf) => {
    scene.add(gltf.scene);
});
```

Each of these loaders provides a callback function that allows you to manipulate the model after it has been loaded, such as adding it to the scene or setting its position and rotation.

Animating Models

Many 3D models come with built-in animations, especially those in the FBX or GLTF formats. In this section, we'll discuss how to animate models in Three.js.

Using Animation Mixers

Three.js provides an AnimationMixer class, which helps manage and play animations. Here's how you can use it:

1. **Load the Model**: Load a model that includes animations, such as a GLTF or FBX file.
2. **Create an Animation Mixer**: Instantiate an AnimationMixer for the loaded model.
3. **Play the Animation**: Use the mixer to play the desired animation.

Here's an example of how to animate a GLTF model:

```javascript
Copy code
let mixer;

gltfLoader.load('path/to/animated-model.gltf', (gltf) => {
    const model = gltf.scene;
    mixer = new THREE.AnimationMixer(model);

    // Get the animation clips and add them to the mixer
    gltf.animations.forEach((clip) => {
        mixer.clipAction(clip).play();
    });

    scene.add(model);
});

// In the animation loop, update the mixer
function animate() {
    requestAnimationFrame(animate);
    if (mixer) mixer.update(0.01); // Update mixer for animations
    renderer.render(scene, camera);
}
animate();
```

This code demonstrates how to load an animated GLTF model and use the AnimationMixer to play its animations. You can manage multiple animations and blend them seamlessly with this approach.

Optimizing Models for Performance

When developing games, performance is paramount, especially in 3D environments where complex models can hinder frame rates. Here are several strategies to optimize your models for better performance:

1. **Reduce Polygon Count**

High-polygon models can significantly impact performance. Aim to simplify your models by reducing their polygon count without compromising visual fidelity. Use tools like Blender or Maya to decimate the model while maintaining its overall shape.

2. **Use Level of Detail (LOD)**

Implementing Level of Detail (LOD) allows you to load different versions of a model based on the camera distance. Use high-detail models when the player is close and lower-detail models when they are far away. Three.js provides a built-in THREE.LOD class to manage this efficiently.

```javascript
Copy code
const lod = new THREE.LOD();
lod.addLevel(highDetailModel, 0);
lod.addLevel(mediumDetailModel, 50);
lod.addLevel(lowDetailModel, 100);
scene.add(lod);
```

3. **Texture Optimization**

Textures can also affect performance, especially high-resolution images. Optimize your textures by:

- **Reducing Resolution**: Scale down the texture resolution where possible.
- **Compressing Textures**: Use formats like JPEG for images or PNG for images with transparency. Additionally, consider using compressed texture formats (like KTX) for better performance on mobile devices.

4. **Batching and Merging Geometries**

Batching or merging geometries can reduce draw calls, improving performance. You can combine multiple meshes with the same material into a single geometry.

```javascript
Copy code
const combinedGeometry =
THREE.BufferGeometryUtils.mergeBufferGeometries([mesh1.geometry,
mesh2.geometry], false);
const combinedMesh = new THREE.Mesh(combinedGeometry, material);
scene.add(combinedMesh);
```

5. Culling Unseen Objects

Culling is a technique where objects outside the camera's view are not rendered. Three.js automatically performs frustum culling, but you can also implement occlusion culling to avoid rendering objects hidden behind others.

In this chapter, we explored how to work with 3D models in Three.js, covering the import process for different formats, techniques for animating models, and optimization strategies to ensure smooth performance. By effectively incorporating 3D models, you can enhance the visual appeal of your game and provide players with a rich, immersive experience.

As you continue your journey in 3D game development, experimenting with various models and animation techniques will further expand your creativity and skill set. In the next chapter, we will delve into more advanced topics, such as implementing particle systems and special effects, to elevate your game's aesthetics and interactivity.

Chapter 7: Environment Creation

C reating engaging 3D environments is a fundamental aspect of game development. The environments not only provide the backdrop for gameplay but also influence player experience and immersion. In this chapter, we will explore techniques for creating diverse 3D terrains, utilizing procedural generation, and incorporating various environmental effects such as skyboxes and water. Here's what we will cover:

1. **Creating 3D Terrains**
2. **Generating Procedural Terrain with Height Maps**
3. **Adding Skyboxes and Environments**
4. **Creating Water and Other Special Effects**

Creating 3D Terrains

Creating realistic 3D terrains involves the use of geometries, textures, and materials to simulate natural landscapes. Whether you're designing mountains, valleys, or plains, the goal is to craft environments that enhance gameplay and draw players into your world.

Basic Terrain Creation

The simplest form of creating a terrain in Three.js is by using geometries. For instance, you can use a plane geometry and manipulate its vertices to create hills and valleys.

Example: Creating a Simple Terrain

```javascript
Copy code
const terrainWidth = 100;
const terrainHeight = 100;
const segments = 100;

const terrainGeometry = new THREE.PlaneGeometry(terrainWidth,
terrainHeight, segments, segments);
const terrainMaterial = new THREE.MeshStandardMaterial({ color:
0x228B22 });

const terrain = new THREE.Mesh(terrainGeometry, terrainMaterial);
terrain.rotation.x = -Math.PI / 2; // Rotate the plane to lie flat
scene.add(terrain);
```

In this example, a PlaneGeometry is created with defined width and height. The number of segments determines the resolution of the terrain. The rotation.x is set to -Math.PI / 2 to lay the plane flat on the ground.

Manipulating Terrain Vertices

To create hills and valleys, you can modify the vertices of the plane geometry. This involves iterating through the geometry's vertices and applying a height function.

Example: Manipulating Vertices for Terrain

```javascript
Copy code
const noise = new SimplexNoise(); // Assuming you have a noise
library
for (let i = 0; i < terrainGeometry.attributes.position.count;
i++) {
    const vertex = terrainGeometry.attributes.position;
    const x = vertex.getX(i);
    const z = vertex.getZ(i);
```

```
    const height = noise.noise2D(x / 10, z / 10) * 5; // Adjust
    height using noise
    vertex.setY(i, height); // Set the new height
}
terrainGeometry.computeVertexNormals(); // Update normals for
lighting
terrainGeometry.attributes.position.needsUpdate = true; // Notify
Three.js to update the geometry
```

In this example, we utilize a noise library like SimplexNoise to generate a more natural, organic-looking terrain. The height is adjusted based on the noise function, giving a more realistic appearance to hills and valleys.

Texturing the Terrain

After shaping the terrain, applying textures is essential to achieve a realistic look. You can use different textures for grass, dirt, rocks, and snow to create a diverse landscape.

Example: Applying Textures

To apply textures, create a THREE.TextureLoader instance and load your desired textures:

```javascript
Copy code
const textureLoader = new THREE.TextureLoader();
const grassTexture = textureLoader.load('path/to/grass.jpg');
grassTexture.wrapS = grassTexture.wrapT = THREE.RepeatWrapping; //
Repeat the texture
grassTexture.repeat.set(10, 10); // Repeat the texture over the
terrain

terrainMaterial.map = grassTexture; // Assign the texture to the
material
terrainMaterial.needsUpdate = true; // Notify Three.js to update
the material
```

By using RepeatWrapping, the texture will repeat across the surface of the terrain, giving it a more natural appearance.

Generating Procedural Terrain with Height Maps

Procedural terrain generation allows developers to create complex landscapes algorithmically, offering flexibility and variability. Height maps, which are grayscale images where the brightness of each pixel represents elevation, can be used to create intricate terrains.

Understanding Height Maps

Height maps use pixel values to determine the height of terrain at various points. A white pixel corresponds to a high elevation, while a black pixel represents low elevation.

Creating a Terrain from a Height Map

To create terrain using a height map, you can load the image as a texture and extract pixel data to adjust the vertices of your terrain mesh.

```javascript
Copy code
const heightMapTexture =
textureLoader.load('path/to/heightmap.png', (texture) => {
    const canvas = document.createElement('canvas');
    const context = canvas.getContext('2d');
    canvas.width = texture.image.width;
    canvas.height = texture.image.height;
    context.drawImage(texture.image, 0, 0);

    const imageData = context.getImageData(0, 0, canvas.width,
    canvas.height);
    const data = imageData.data;

    for (let i = 0; i < terrainGeometry.attributes.position.count;
    i++) {
        const vertex = terrainGeometry.attributes.position;
        const x = Math.floor(vertex.getX(i) + terrainWidth / 2);
```

```
        const z = Math.floor(vertex.getZ(i) + terrainHeight / 2);

        // Ensure x and z are within bounds
        if (x >= 0 && x < canvas.width && z >= 0 && z <
        canvas.height) {
            const pixelIndex = (z * canvas.width + x) * 4; // 4
            for RGBA
            const height = data[pixelIndex] / 255; // Normalized
            height (0-1)
            vertex.setY(i, height * 10); // Scale height
        }
    }

    terrainGeometry.attributes.position.needsUpdate = true; //
    Notify Three.js to update the geometry
    terrainGeometry.computeVertexNormals(); // Update normals for
    lighting
});
```

In this example, we load a height map texture, extract pixel data, and use it to adjust the vertices of the terrain. The heights are normalized to create a more visually appealing landscape.

Optimizing Procedural Terrain

Procedural terrain generation can be resource-intensive. Here are some techniques to optimize performance:

1. **Level of Detail (LOD)**: Use different resolutions for terrains based on the camera distance. Farther terrains can use lower-resolution meshes to reduce the number of polygons rendered.
2. **Chunking**: Divide the terrain into chunks that load and unload based on the player's position, reducing the load on the GPU.
3. **Vertex Compression**: Reduce the amount of data sent to the GPU by using lower precision for vertex positions when high precision is unnecessary.

Adding Skyboxes and Environments

Skyboxes create the illusion of distant landscapes and skies, enriching the visual experience of your game. A skybox typically consists of a cube with textures mapped to its sides.

Creating a Skybox

To create a skybox in Three.js, you can use a THREE.BoxGeometry and apply textures to each face.

Example: Creating a Simple Skybox

```javascript
Copy code
const skyboxGeometry = new THREE.BoxGeometry(1000, 1000, 1000);
const skyboxMaterials = [
    new THREE.MeshBasicMaterial({ map:
    textureLoader.load('path/to/px.jpg'), side: THREE.BackSide }),
    // Positive X
    new THREE.MeshBasicMaterial({ map:
    textureLoader.load('path/to/nx.jpg'), side: THREE.BackSide }),
    // Negative X
    new THREE.MeshBasicMaterial({ map:
    textureLoader.load('path/to/py.jpg'), side: THREE.BackSide }),
    // Positive Y
    new THREE.MeshBasicMaterial({ map:
    textureLoader.load('path/to/ny.jpg'), side: THREE.BackSide }),
    // Negative Y
    new THREE.MeshBasicMaterial({ map:
    textureLoader.load('path/to/pz.jpg'), side: THREE.BackSide }),
    // Positive Z
    new THREE.MeshBasicMaterial({ map:
    textureLoader.load('path/to/nz.jpg'), side: THREE.BackSide }),
    // Negative Z
];

const skybox = new THREE.Mesh(skyboxGeometry, skyboxMaterials);
```

```
scene.add(skybox);
```

In this example, we create a skybox by mapping textures to the inside of a cube. Using THREE.BackSide ensures that the textures are rendered from the inside, making it appear as if the player is surrounded by the sky.

Using Skyboxes for Dynamic Environments

You can enhance the immersion of your game by creating dynamic skyboxes that change based on the time of day or weather conditions. This can be accomplished by swapping textures in the skybox material or adjusting the skybox's color based on game events.

Adding Environmental Effects

In addition to skyboxes, you can further enhance your environment with effects like fog, atmospheric scattering, and volumetric clouds. These elements can help create a more immersive experience.

Example: Adding Fog

To add fog to your scene, you can set the fog property of the scene:

```javascript
Copy code
scene.fog = new THREE.FogExp2(0xaaaaaa, 0.1); // Color and density
```

This example creates an exponential fog effect that can create depth and atmosphere in your scene.

Creating Water and Other Special Effects

Water is a crucial element in many games, providing realistic interactions and aesthetics. In Three.js, you can create water surfaces that reflect the environment and simulate waves.

Creating a Basic Water Surface

Using the THREE.Water class from the three/examples/jsm/ directory, you can create a realistic water surface.

Example: Creating Water with Three.js

```javascript
Copy code
import { Water } from 'three/examples/jsm/objects/Water.js';

const waterGeometry = new THREE.PlaneGeometry(100, 100);
const water = new Water(water

const waterMaterial = new Water(waterGeometry, {
    color: 0x001e0f,
    scale: 4,
    flowDirection: new THREE.Vector2(1, 1),
    textureWidth: 1024,
    textureHeight: 1024,
});

const waterMesh = new THREE.Mesh(waterGeometry, waterMaterial);
waterMesh.rotation.x = -Math.PI / 2; // Rotate the water to lie
flat
scene.add(waterMesh);
```

In this example, we create a water surface using THREE.Water, which allows for realistic wave simulation and reflections. The water color, scale, flow direction, and texture resolution can be adjusted to achieve the desired look.

Adding Reflection and Refraction

One of the most visually appealing features of water is its ability to reflect and refract its environment. You can achieve this effect by passing a camera and other scene parameters to the water material.

Example: Adding Reflection and Refraction

```
javascript
Copy code
waterMaterial.reflectivity = 0.5; // Adjust for desired reflection
intensity
waterMaterial.refractionRatio = 0.9; // Control refraction strength
```

The reflectivity property determines how much of the environment is reflected on the water's surface, while refractionRatio affects the bending of light as it passes through the water.

Special Effects: Particles and Volumetric Fog

In addition to water, you can enhance your environments with particle systems and volumetric fog to simulate various effects like rain, snow, and dust.

Example: Adding a Particle System for Rain

```
javascript
Copy code
const particleCount = 1000;
const particles = new THREE.BufferGeometry();
const positions = new Float32Array(particleCount * 3);

for (let i = 0; i < particleCount; i++) {
    positions[i * 3] = Math.random() * terrainWidth - terrainWidth
    / 2; // X
    positions[i * 3 + 1] = Math.random() * terrainHeight + 50; //
    Y (start above the terrain)
    positions[i * 3 + 2] = Math.random() * terrainHeight -
    terrainHeight / 2; // Z
}

particles.setAttribute('position', new
THREE.BufferAttribute(positions, 3));
const particleMaterial = new THREE.PointsMaterial({ color:
0x888888 });
```

```
const particleSystem = new THREE.Points(particles,
particleMaterial);
scene.add(particleSystem);
```

This example creates a simple rain effect by generating random positions for particles above the terrain. The PointsMaterial gives them a basic appearance, but you can enhance this further by adding textures or adjusting the opacity.

Volumetric Fog Example

To simulate volumetric fog, you can create a plane geometry and use a shader material that calculates the fog density based on distance from the camera.

```javascript
Copy code
const fogGeometry = new THREE.PlaneGeometry(1000, 1000);
const fogMaterial = new THREE.ShaderMaterial({
    uniforms: {
        fogDensity: { value: 0.05 },
        cameraPosition: { value: camera.position },
    },
    vertexShader: `
        varying vec3 vWorldPosition;
        void main() {
            vec4 worldPosition = modelMatrix * vec4(position, 1.0);
            vWorldPosition = worldPosition.xyz;
            gl_Position = projectionMatrix * viewMatrix *
            worldPosition;
        }
    `,
    fragmentShader: `
        uniform float fogDensity;
        varying vec3 vWorldPosition;
        void main() {
            float distance = length(vWorldPosition);
            float fogFactor = exp(-distance * fogDensity);
            gl_FragColor = vec4(1.0, 1.0, 1.0, 1.0) * fogFactor;
```

```
    }
     `,
});
const fogMesh = new THREE.Mesh(fogGeometry, fogMaterial);
fogMesh.position.set(0, 0, 0); // Position the fog mesh as desired
scene.add(fogMesh);
```

In this example, we create a fog mesh that gradually fades out based on distance from the camera. This simulates a sense of depth and enhances the atmosphere of the scene.

In this chapter, we covered various techniques for creating immersive 3D environments. We started with basic terrain creation using geometries and textures, moving on to procedural terrain generation using height maps. We then explored the addition of skyboxes and dynamic environments, enhancing the game's visual appeal.

Finally, we discussed creating realistic water effects and adding special effects like particle systems and volumetric fog. By mastering these techniques, you can create rich, engaging worlds that draw players into your 3D games and elevate the overall gaming experience.

As we proceed to the next chapters, we will delve deeper into game mechanics, interactivity, and further enhancements to make your 3D game more dynamic and engaging.

Chapter 8: Building Game Mechanics

uilding a successful game is about more than just stunning graphics and captivating environments; it requires a solid foundation of game mechanics that engage players and provide a seamless gameplay experience. This chapter focuses on critical game mechanics, including managing game states, implementing player movement and controls, collision detection and response, and integrating health systems, scores, and objectives. By the end of this chapter, you will have the tools to create a functional game that offers players an immersive experience.

Game States: Starting, Running, and Pausing the Game

Game states define the various stages of a game and how the player interacts with it. Typically, a game will have at least three primary states: starting, running, and pausing.

1. Understanding Game States

- **Starting State:** This is where the game initializes. In this state, you will often display a main menu or a loading screen and set up the game environment, resources, and variables.
- **Running State:** In this state, the game is actively playing, with mechanics like player movement, physics, and game rules being processed. It encompasses the majority of gameplay, where players will interact with the game world.

- **Paused State:** This allows players to take a break without losing their progress. In this state, the game typically stops processing inputs and updates, but the current game state is preserved.

2. Implementing Game States

To manage these states in Three.js, we can create an object to hold the current state and use it to control the game flow.

Example: Managing Game States

```javascript
Copy code
const gameStates = {
    STARTING: 'starting',
    RUNNING: 'running',
    PAUSED: 'paused',
};

let currentState = gameStates.STARTING;

function updateGame() {
    if (currentState === gameStates.RUNNING) {
        // Update game logic and rendering
    }
}

function startGame() {
    currentState = gameStates.RUNNING;
    // Initialize game elements and start the game loop
}

function pauseGame() {
    currentState = gameStates.PAUSED;
    // Stop game updates
}

function resumeGame() {
    currentState = gameStates.RUNNING;
```

```
    // Resume game updates
}
```

In this example, we define our game states in an object and set the currentState variable accordingly. The updateGame function checks the current state and performs updates only when the game is running.

3. Transitioning Between States

Transitioning between these states can be triggered by user inputs or specific events in the game. For instance, pressing the 'Start' button will transition from the starting state to the running state, while pressing 'Escape' might pause the game.

Example: Handling State Transitions

```javascript
Copy code
document.addEventListener('keydown', (event) => {
    if (event.key === 'Enter' && currentState ===
    gameStates.STARTING) {
        startGame();
    }
    if (event.key === 'Escape' && currentState ===
    gameStates.RUNNING) {
        pauseGame();
    }
    if (event.key === 'Escape' && currentState ===
    gameStates.PAUSED) {
        resumeGame();
    }
});
```

In this example, we listen for key presses to transition between states, allowing the player to start, pause, or resume the game.

Implementing Player Movement and Controls

Player movement is one of the most critical aspects of game mechanics. It creates the foundation for interaction and gameplay.

1. Setting Up Player Controls

We can implement player controls using keyboard inputs or mouse movements. For this example, we'll focus on keyboard controls for a simple player object.

Example: Basic Player Movement

```javascript
Copy code
const player = new THREE.Mesh(new THREE.BoxGeometry(1, 1, 1), new
THREE.MeshBasicMaterial({ color: 0x00ff00 }));
scene.add(player);

const moveSpeed = 0.1;

function handlePlayerMovement() {
    document.addEventListener('keydown', (event) => {
        switch (event.key) {
            case 'ArrowUp':
                player.position.z -= moveSpeed; // Move forward
                break;
            case 'ArrowDown':
                player.position.z += moveSpeed; // Move backward
                break;
            case 'ArrowLeft':
                player.position.x -= moveSpeed; // Move left
                break;
            case 'ArrowRight':
                player.position.x += moveSpeed; // Move right
                break;
        }
    });
```

```
}
```

In this example, we create a basic player object (a green box) and handle movement based on arrow key inputs. The handlePlayerMovement function listens for keydown events and updates the player's position accordingly.

2. Advanced Player Controls

To create a more immersive experience, consider implementing features like sprinting, jumping, and camera follow.

Example: Adding Sprint and Jump Mechanics

```javascript
javascript
Copy code
let isJumping = false;

document.addEventListener('keydown', (event) => {
    if (event.key === 'Shift') {
        moveSpeed *= 2; // Sprint
    }
    if (event.key === 'Space' && !isJumping) {
        isJumping = true;
        player.position.y += 2; // Jump effect
        setTimeout(() => {
            player.position.y -= 2; // Return to original position
            isJumping = false;
        }, 500); // Jump duration
    }
});

document.addEventListener('keyup', (event) => {
    if (event.key === 'Shift') {
        moveSpeed /= 2; // Stop sprinting
    }
});
```

In this enhanced example, holding the Shift key doubles the player's movement speed, while pressing the Spacebar allows the player to jump.

3. Camera Control

For a more immersive experience, you may want to follow the player with the camera.

Example: Camera Follow

```javascript
Copy code
function updateCamera() {
    camera.position.x = player.position.x;
    camera.position.z = player.position.z + 5; // Keep camera
    behind the player
    camera.lookAt(player.position);
}
```

The updateCamera function positions the camera based on the player's position, providing a third-person perspective.

Collision Detection and Response

Collision detection is vital in most games, as it helps to determine when two objects interact. In 3D games, this often involves checking whether a player's bounding box intersects with other objects in the game world.

1. Understanding Bounding Boxes

Three.js provides built-in methods for collision detection using bounding boxes or bounding spheres. A bounding box encapsulates an object, allowing for simple collision checks.

Example: Checking for Collisions

```javascript
Copy code
const playerBox = new THREE.Box3().setFromObject(player);
const enemyBox = new THREE.Box3().setFromObject(enemy);
```

```
if (playerBox.intersectsBox(enemyBox)) {
    // Handle collision (e.g., reduce health)
}
```

In this example, we create bounding boxes for both the player and an enemy object and check for intersections. If they intersect, we can implement a response, such as reducing the player's health.

2. Implementing Collision Responses

After detecting a collision, you need to define how the game will respond. This can vary from reducing health to triggering an animation or sound effect.

Example: Reducing Health on Collision

```javascript
Copy code
let playerHealth = 100;

if (playerBox.intersectsBox(enemyBox)) {
    playerHealth -= 10; // Reduce health
    console.log(`Player health: ${playerHealth}`);
}
```

In this case, if a collision occurs, we reduce the player's health by 10 and log the current health.

3. More Advanced Collision Techniques

For more complex games, consider implementing physics engines like **Cannon.js** or **Ammo.js**, which provide robust collision detection and response systems.

Adding Health, Scores, and Game Objectives

An engaging game requires a system to track player health, scores, and objectives, providing motivation and feedback during gameplay.

1. Health System

Implementing a health system allows players to know their status and adds tension to gameplay.

Example: Health Display

```javascript
Copy code
const healthDisplay = document.getElementById('healthDisplay');

function updateHealthDisplay() {
    healthDisplay.innerText = `Health: ${playerHealth}`;
}
```

This example updates the health display in the user interface to show the current health.

2. Scoring System

A scoring system encourages players to achieve objectives and compete against others. You can track scores based on various actions, like defeating enemies or collecting items.

Example: Basic Scoring System

```javascript
Copy code
let score = 0;

function addScore(points) {
```

```javascript
        score += points;
        console.log(`Score: ${score}`);
    }
```

Whenever a player accomplishes an objective, such as collecting an item or defeating an enemy, you can call addScore to update their score.

3. Game Objectives

Setting clear objectives guides players through the game. These can include tasks such as collecting a certain number of items, reaching a specific location, or defeating a boss.

 Example: Defining Game Objectives

```javascript
javascript
Copy code
const objectives = [
    { description: 'Collect 10 coins', completed: false, goal: 10,
    current: 0 },
];

function updateObjectives(itemCollected) {
    if (itemCollected) {
        objectives[0].current += 1;
        if (objectives[0].current >= objectives[0].goal) {
            objectives[0].completed = true;
            console.log('Objective completed!');
        }
    }
}
```

In this example, we define an objective for collecting coins. The updateObjectives function checks whether the player has collected a coin and updates the objective status accordingly.

 In this chapter, we explored the essential components of game mechanics, including managing game states, implementing player movement and controls, and handling collision detection and responses. We also discussed integrating health, scores, and objectives to create a compelling gameplay experience.

As you build your game, remember that mechanics should feel intuitive and responsive to keep players engaged. The next chapters will delve into creating more advanced game systems, including enemy AI and level progression, to further enhance your 3D game development skills.

Chapter 9: Adding Physics to Your Game

Incorporating physics into your 3D game enhances realism and engagement, providing players with a more immersive experience. Physics engines simulate real-world physics, such as gravity, collisions, and movement, allowing for dynamic interactions within your game environment. This chapter will introduce you to physics engines, specifically Cannon.js and Ammo.js, and guide you through implementing rigid bodies, forces, gravity, collision detection, and physics-based interactions.

Introduction to Physics Engines: Cannon.js and Ammo.js

1. What Are Physics Engines?

Physics engines are software frameworks that simulate physical systems, allowing developers to create realistic interactions between objects in a game. They handle calculations for movement, collision detection, and forces, enabling game developers to focus on gameplay rather than complex mathematical equations.

2. Choosing a Physics Engine

When it comes to 3D game development with JavaScript, two popular physics engines are **Cannon.js** and **Ammo.js**. Each has its strengths, and the choice depends on your game's requirements.

- **Cannon.js**: A lightweight and easy-to-use physics engine that is well-suited for 2D and 3D games. It offers a simple API for defining physics properties and simulating basic interactions.
- **Ammo.js**: A port of the Bullet physics engine to JavaScript. It is more feature-rich and can handle complex simulations, including rigid body dynamics, soft body physics, and character controllers.

3. Setting Up a Physics Engine

To use Cannon.js or Ammo.js in your game, you need to include the library in your project. Below are the steps for both engines:

Setting Up Cannon.js

1. **Installation**: You can install Cannon.js using npm or include it directly in your HTML file.

```html
Copy code
<script
src="https://cdnjs.cloudflare.com/ajax/libs/cannon-es/0.19.0/
cannon-es.min.js"></script>
```

1. **Initialization**: Create a physics world.

```javascript
Copy code
const world = new CANNON.World();
world.gravity.set(0, -9.82, 0); // Gravity in the Y direction
```

Setting Up Ammo.js

1. **Installation**: Similar to Cannon.js, you can use npm or include it directly in your HTML.

```html
html
Copy code
<script
src="https://cdn.rawgit.com/kripken/ammo.js/master/builds/ammo.js"
></script>
```

1. **Initialization**: Create an Ammo physics world.

```javascript
javascript
Copy code
Ammo().then((Ammo) => {
    const collisionConfiguration = new
    Ammo.btDefaultCollisionConfiguration();
    const dispatcher = new
    Ammo.btCollisionDispatcher(collisionConfiguration);
    const broadphase = new Ammo.btDbvtBroadphase();
    const solver = new Ammo.btSequentialImpulseConstraintSolver();
    const physicsWorld = new
    Ammo.btDiscreteDynamicsWorld(dispatcher, broadphase, solver,
    collisionConfiguration);
    physicsWorld.setGravity(new Ammo.btVector3(0, -9.82, 0));
});
```

Rigid Bodies and Forces

1. Understanding Rigid Bodies

In physics engines, a **rigid body** is an object that does not deform when forces are applied. Rigid bodies can move, rotate, and collide with other rigid bodies, allowing for realistic interactions in your game.

2. Creating Rigid Bodies in Cannon.js

To create a rigid body in Cannon.js, you need to define its shape, mass, and position. Below is an example of how to create a simple box and add it to the physics world.

Example: Creating a Box Rigid Body

```javascript
Copy code
const boxShape = new CANNON.Box(new CANNON.Vec3(1, 1, 1)); // Box
shape with dimensions 2x2x2
const boxBody = new CANNON.Body({
    mass: 1, // Mass of the box
    position: new CANNON.Vec3(0, 5, 0), // Initial position
});

// Add the box shape to the body
boxBody.addShape(boxShape);

// Add the body to the physics world
world.addBody(boxBody);
```

3. Applying Forces to Rigid Bodies

You can apply forces and impulses to rigid bodies to simulate movement. Forces are continuously applied, while impulses are instantaneous.

Example: Applying a Force

```javascript
Copy code
const force = new CANNON.Vec3(0, 10, 0); // Force vector pointing
upward
boxBody.applyForce(force, boxBody.position); // Apply force at the
center of the box
```

Gravity and Collision Detection

1. Implementing Gravity

Gravity is a fundamental aspect of physics simulation. It affects all rigid bodies within the physics world. In both Cannon.js and Ammo.js, you can set the gravity vector for the world, which will automatically affect all objects.

Example: Setting Gravity in Cannon.js

As shown earlier, you set gravity during the initialization of the world:

```javascript
Copy code
world.gravity.set(0, -9.82, 0); // Gravity in the Y direction
```

2. Collision Detection

Collision detection is the process of identifying when two objects intersect. Both Cannon.js and Ammo.js handle collision detection internally, but you can subscribe to collision events to implement custom behavior.

Example: Collision Detection in Cannon.js

You can use the postStep event to check for collisions after the physics simulation step:

```javascript
Copy code
world.addEventListener('postStep', () => {
    // Check for collisions
    world.bodies.forEach(body => {
        if (body.position.y < 0) {
            // Handle the object falling below the ground
            world.remove(body); // Remove the body from the world
        }
    });
```

```
});
```

3. Handling Collisions

To handle collisions effectively, you can implement collision callbacks. In Cannon.js, you can use the collide event to respond to specific interactions.

Example: Handling Collisions in Cannon.js

```javascript
Copy code
world.addEventListener('collide', (event) => {
    const { bodyA, bodyB } = event;
    if (bodyA === boxBody || bodyB === boxBody) {
        console.log('Collision detected with box!');
    }
});
```

Creating Physics-Based Interactions

1. Designing Interactive Elements

Adding physics-based interactions allows players to engage with the game world more meaningfully. This could include pushing objects, bouncing off surfaces, or triggering events based on collisions.

2. Creating Interactive Objects

You can create interactive objects that respond to player input or environmental factors.

Example: Pushing a Box

You can simulate pushing a box by applying a force when the player interacts with it.

```javascript
Copy code
document.addEventListener('keydown', (event) => {
    if (event.key === 'P') {
        // Apply a force to push the box
        boxBody.applyForce(new CANNON.Vec3(5, 0, 0),
        boxBody.position);
    }
});
```

3. Simulating Bouncing Objects

Physics engines can simulate bouncing by adjusting the restitution property of rigid bodies, which determines how bouncy an object is when it collides with another object.

  Example: Bouncy Box

```javascript
Copy code
boxBody.material = new CANNON.Material();
boxBody.restitution = 0.8; // Set high restitution for bouncing
```

4. Triggering Events Based on Collisions

You can create game mechanics that respond to specific collisions, such as activating traps, opening doors, or changing game states.

  Example: Activating an Event on Collision

```javascript
Copy code
world.addEventListener('collide', (event) => {
    const { bodyA, bodyB } = event;
```

```
    if (bodyA === playerBody && bodyB === trapBody) {
        // Trigger trap activation
        console.log('Trap activated!');
        // Perform trap logic (e.g., reduce health)
    }
});
```

Adding physics to your 3D game elevates the gameplay experience, allowing for dynamic and interactive environments. By utilizing physics engines like Cannon.js and Ammo.js, you can create realistic interactions, handle gravity and collisions, and implement engaging game mechanics.

In this chapter, we explored the basics of physics engines, created rigid bodies, applied forces, implemented gravity and collision detection, and designed physics-based interactions. As you continue your game development journey, consider how physics can enhance your game's realism and engagement, leading to a richer player experience.

In the upcoming chapters, we will delve into more advanced topics, such as implementing enemy AI, level progression, and enhancing the overall gameplay experience through effective game design and mechanics.

Chapter 10: Creating Characters and NPCs

Characters and non-player characters (NPCs) are integral elements of any 3D game. They serve as the driving force behind player interaction, narrative development, and gameplay mechanics. This chapter will guide you through the process of designing and animating player characters, adding NPCs, implementing basic AI for NPCs, and creating dialogue and interaction systems. By the end of this chapter, you'll have a comprehensive understanding of how to create engaging characters that enhance your game's world.

Designing and Animating Player Characters

1. Character Design Fundamentals

The design of a character sets the tone for your game and influences player experience. Here are some fundamental principles to consider when designing your player character:

- **Silhouette**: A strong silhouette makes a character instantly recognizable. Ensure that the shape of your character stands out and reflects their personality.
- **Proportions**: Consider the character's proportions in relation to the game world. A realistic character might have human-like proportions,

while a stylized character could exaggerate features.

- **Color and Texture**: Colors convey emotions and attributes. Bright colors might signify a friendly character, while darker colors may suggest mystery or danger. Textures enhance realism and can indicate a character's background.

2. Modeling Your Character

Character modeling involves creating a 3D representation of your character using a 3D modeling tool such as Blender, Maya, or 3ds Max. Here's a basic workflow for character modeling:

1. **Concept Art**: Start with sketches and concept art to visualize your character. This helps refine ideas before diving into 3D modeling.
2. **Base Mesh**: Create a base mesh that defines the overall shape of your character. This can be done using primitive shapes as building blocks.
3. **Detailing**: Add details such as facial features, clothing, and accessories. Use sculpting tools to create realistic features.
4. **UV Mapping**: Unwrap your model to create a UV map, which is essential for texturing. This process allows textures to be applied accurately to the 3D surface.
5. **Texturing**: Use texture painting tools or software like Substance Painter to create textures that define the surface properties of your model, such as color, bump, and specular maps.

3. Rigging and Skinning

After creating your character model, you need to rig it for animation. Rigging involves creating a skeleton that defines how the character moves. Skinning binds the 3D model to the rig so that the mesh deforms correctly during animations.

Rigging Process:

1. **Create Bones**: Set up a skeleton structure within your 3D modeling software.

2. **Weight Painting**: Assign weights to different parts of the mesh, determining how much influence each bone has on specific vertices.

3. **Testing**: Pose your character using the rig to ensure that the skinning works correctly and that the mesh deforms as expected.

4. Animating Your Character

Character animation brings your character to life. Here are the steps to create animations for your player character:

Animation Techniques:

- **Keyframe Animation**: This technique involves setting keyframes for specific poses and allowing the software to interpolate between them.
- **Motion Capture**: Capture real-life movements using motion capture technology, which can be applied to your character for realistic animations.
- **Procedural Animation**: Use algorithms to generate animations based on physics or game logic, allowing for dynamic movements.

Example: Creating a Simple Walk Cycle

1. **Set Keyframes**: Create keyframes for the contact, down, passing, and up positions of the walk cycle.

2. **Add In-Betweens**: Insert in-between frames to smooth out the animation.

3. **Playback and Refine**: Play back the animation to check for fluidity and make adjustments as needed.

5. Exporting Character Animations

Once your animations are complete, export them in a format compatible with your game engine (e.g., GLTF, FBX). Make sure to include the rig and animation data during export.

Adding Non-Player Characters (NPCs)

1. Defining NPC Roles

NPCs can serve various roles in a game, from quest-givers to enemies or allies. Define the purpose of your NPCs within the game world to ensure they contribute meaningfully to the gameplay experience.

2. Modeling NPCs

The modeling process for NPCs is similar to that of player characters. However, NPCs may not require the same level of detail as player characters, especially if they appear in the background.

3. Rigging and Animation

Follow the same rigging and animation techniques as with player characters, but consider creating a variety of animations for different NPC behaviors (e.g., idle, walking, running, interacting).

4. Adding NPCs to Your Game

To add NPCs to your game, you will need to import their models and animations into your game engine (e.g., Three.js, Unity). Position the NPCs in your game world, ensuring they interact with the environment and player effectively.

Basic AI for NPCs: Movement, Pathfinding, and Behavior Trees

1. Introduction to NPC AI

NPC AI determines how non-player characters interact with the game world and the player. Basic AI can enhance immersion and create engaging gameplay experiences.

2. Movement and Navigation

Basic Movement

Implement basic movement behavior for NPCs, such as walking, running, and idling. This can be achieved through animation blending based on the NPC's state.

Pathfinding

Pathfinding is crucial for NPCs to navigate complex environments. Common algorithms include:

- *A Algorithm**: A widely used pathfinding algorithm that finds the shortest path between two points on a grid.
- **NavMesh**: A predefined mesh that outlines walkable areas in your game world. NPCs can navigate these areas efficiently.

Example: Implementing Basic Pathfinding

1. **Define Walkable Areas**: Create a grid or NavMesh representing walkable terrain.
2. **Pathfinding Algorithm**: Implement the A* algorithm or use an existing library to calculate paths.
3. **Movement**: Move the NPC along the calculated path using interpolation for smooth movement.

3. Behavior Trees

Behavior trees are a hierarchical structure that organizes NPC actions and decisions. They allow for complex behaviors while remaining easy to manage.
  Basic Structure of a Behavior Tree

- **Root Node**: The starting point of the tree that initiates behavior checks.
- **Selector Node**: A node that tries its children in order and succeeds when one child succeeds.
- **Sequence Node**: A node that executes its children in order and succeeds only if all children succeed.
- **Leaf Nodes**: These are the actions or conditions that the NPC can execute or check.

Example: Creating a Simple Behavior Tree

1. **Define Actions**: Create actions for the NPC, such as Patrol, Chase, and Idle.
2. **Structure**: Organize these actions in a tree structure to dictate behavior based on player proximity.
3. **Execution**: Implement a system that updates the behavior tree each frame to evaluate and execute the appropriate actions.

Dialogue and Interaction Systems

1. Importance of Dialogue Systems

Dialogue systems facilitate communication between the player and NPCs, enhancing narrative and gameplay. They can range from simple text prompts to complex branching dialogues.

2. Designing a Dialogue System

Basic Dialogue Structure

1. **Dialogue Tree**: Create a tree structure that outlines the flow of conversation. Each node represents a dialogue option or statement.
2. **Player Choices**: Allow players to choose responses, which can lead to different dialogue branches.
3. **Triggering Events**: Dialogue can trigger specific events in the game, such as quests or NPC reactions.

Example: Implementing a Simple Dialogue System

1. **Define Dialogue**: Create a JSON or XML file containing dialogue nodes and options.

```json
Copy code
{
    "dialogue": [
        {
            "id": 1,
            "text": "Hello, adventurer! How can I help you today?",
            "responses": [
                { "text": "I'm looking for a quest.", "next": 2 },
                { "text": "Just passing by.", "next": 3 }
            ]
        },
        {
            "id": 2,
            "text": "I have a task for you! Defeat the goblin
            king.",
            "responses": []
        },
        {
```

```
        "id": 3,
        "text": "Safe travels!",
        "responses": []
    }
  ]
}
```

1. **Display Dialogue**: Create a function to display the dialogue and options to the player.
2. **Handle Player Choices**: Implement logic to manage player choices and navigate the dialogue tree based on responses.

3. Interaction Systems

Interaction systems define how players engage with NPCs and the environment. This can include picking up items, starting quests, or initiating conversations.

Example: Implementing an Interaction System

1. **Detect Proximity**: Use raycasting or collision detection to check if the player is close enough to interact with an NPC.
2. **Display Interaction Prompt**: Show a prompt when the player is within range (e.g., "Press E to talk").
3. **Trigger Interaction**: When the player interacts, initiate the dialogue system or event.

Creating characters and NPCs is a vital aspect of 3D game development. Through thoughtful design, animation, AI implementation, and interaction systems, you can bring your game world to life, providing players with engaging and immersive experiences.

In this chapter, we explored character design fundamentals, modeling, rigging, and animating player characters, adding NPCs, implementing basic AI for NPCs, and creating dialogue and interaction systems. These elements are essential for crafting a rich, interactive world that captivates players and enhances gameplay. As you continue your game development journey, remember that well-designed characters and NPCs can significantly impact your game's narrative and player engagement.

Chapter 11: Advanced Materials and Shaders

In the realm of 3D game development, visual fidelity plays a crucial role in engaging players and creating immersive experiences. Advanced materials and shaders are essential tools for achieving stunning graphics that elevate your game from good to exceptional. This chapter will delve into the world of shaders, specifically focusing on GLSL (OpenGL Shading Language), how to create custom shaders in Three.js, post-processing effects such as bloom and motion blur, and the implementation of particle systems. By the end of this chapter, you will possess a robust understanding of advanced materials and shaders, enabling you to enhance the visual quality of your 3D game.

Introduction to Shaders and GLSL

What Are Shaders?

Shaders are small programs that run on the GPU (Graphics Processing Unit) to determine how vertices and pixels are rendered in a scene. They allow developers to manipulate the rendering pipeline, providing the ability to create intricate visual effects that would be impossible with fixed-function graphics pipelines. Shaders can control aspects such as lighting, texture mapping, color blending, and more.

Types of Shaders

1. **Vertex Shaders**: These shaders process vertex data and perform operations such as transformations (positioning, scaling, and rotating) and lighting calculations. Vertex shaders are the first stage in the graphics pipeline.

2. **Fragment Shaders**: Also known as pixel shaders, these shaders calculate the color of each pixel rendered on the screen. They take data from vertex shaders and apply textures, lighting, and other effects to produce the final pixel color.

3. **Geometry Shaders**: These shaders can generate new geometry from existing vertex data. They operate between the vertex and fragment shaders and can be used for effects like dynamic shadow mapping or generating additional details.

Understanding GLSL (OpenGL Shading Language)

GLSL is a high-level shading language used to write shaders for OpenGL, which is the underlying graphics API utilized by Three.js. GLSL is designed to be simple and efficient, providing a C-like syntax that is easy to learn for programmers familiar with similar languages. Here are some basic concepts of GLSL:

- **Variables**: GLSL supports various data types, including floats, integers, vectors (vec2, vec3, vec4), and matrices. These are used to store and manipulate data within shaders.
- **Built-in Functions**: GLSL provides numerous built-in functions for mathematical operations, texture sampling, and other utilities, enabling developers to create complex effects easily.
- **Precision Qualifiers**: GLSL allows developers to specify precision for variables, which can affect performance and rendering quality. Common qualifiers include highp, mediump, and lowp.

A Simple Vertex and Fragment Shader Example

Here's a basic example of a vertex shader and a fragment shader that renders a colored triangle.

Vertex Shader:

```glsl
Copy code
#version 300 es
layout(location = 0) in vec4 position;
layout(location = 1) in vec3 color;
out vec3 fragColor;

void main() {
    gl_Position = position; // Transform the vertex position
    fragColor = color; // Pass the color to the fragment shader
}
```

Fragment Shader:

```glsl
Copy code
#version 300 es
precision mediump float;
in vec3 fragColor;
out vec4 outColor;

void main() {
    outColor = vec4(fragColor, 1.0); // Set the pixel color
}
```

In this example, the vertex shader receives position and color attributes, transforms the position, and passes the color to the fragment shader, which outputs the final pixel color.

Creating Custom Shaders in Three.js

Three.js simplifies the process of using shaders by providing built-in functionality for creating and managing custom shaders. Below is a step-by-step guide to creating and using custom shaders in Three.js.

Step 1: Setting Up Your Scene

Before creating custom shaders, ensure you have a basic Three.js scene set up with a camera, renderer, and a light source.

```javascript
Copy code
// Basic Three.js scene setup
const scene = new THREE.Scene();
const camera = new THREE.PerspectiveCamera(75, window.innerWidth /
window.innerHeight, 0.1, 1000);
const renderer = new THREE.WebGLRenderer();
renderer.setSize(window.innerWidth, window.innerHeight);
document.body.appendChild(renderer.domElement);

// Add a light source
const light = new THREE.PointLight(0xffffff);
light.position.set(10, 10, 10);
scene.add(light);
```

Step 2: Creating Custom Shaders

To create a custom shader material, define the vertex and fragment shader codes. You can use the THREE.ShaderMaterial class to combine these shaders and apply them to your mesh.

```javascript
Copy code
```

```
const vertexShader = `
    varying vec3 vColor;

    void main() {
        vColor = vec3(1.0, 0.5, 0.0); // Set a constant color
        gl_Position = projectionMatrix * modelViewMatrix *
        vec4(position, 1.0);
    }
`;

const fragmentShader = `
    varying vec3 vColor;

    void main() {
        gl_FragColor = vec4(vColor, 1.0); // Use the interpolated
        color
    }
`;

const shaderMaterial = new THREE.ShaderMaterial({
    vertexShader,
    fragmentShader,
});
```

Step 3: Creating and Adding a Mesh

Now, create a geometry and apply the custom shader material to it. In this
example, we'll create a simple cube.

```javascript
Copy code
const geometry = new THREE.BoxGeometry();
const cube = new THREE.Mesh(geometry, shaderMaterial);
scene.add(cube);
```

Step 4: Rendering the Scene

Finally, create a render loop to continuously render the scene and animate the cube.

```javascript
Copy code
function animate() {
    requestAnimationFrame(animate);
    cube.rotation.x += 0.01; // Rotate the cube
    cube.rotation.y += 0.01;
    renderer.render(scene, camera);
}
animate();
```

This code will create a rotating cube that utilizes your custom shaders, rendering it with the specified color.

Post-Processing Effects: Bloom, Motion Blur, and Depth of Field

Post-processing effects are techniques applied to the final rendered image to enhance visual quality. Three.js provides an easy way to implement post-processing effects using the EffectComposer class.

Setting Up Post-Processing

1. **Install Necessary Libraries**: Ensure you have the Three.js post-processing library installed. If you haven't already, you can include it in your project.
2. **Create an Effect Composer**:

```javascript
Copy code
const composer = new THREE.EffectComposer(renderer);
composer.addPass(new THREE.RenderPass(scene, camera));
```

Bloom Effect

The bloom effect simulates the way bright lights bleed into surrounding areas, creating a soft glow.

1. **Add the Bloom Pass**:

```javascript
Copy code
const bloomPass = new THREE.UnrealBloomPass(new
THREE.Vector2(window.innerWidth, window.innerHeight), 1.5, 0.4,
0.85);
composer.addPass(bloomPass);
```

1. **Render the Composer**:

Replace the render call in your animation loop with the composer's render method:

```javascript
Copy code
function animate() {
    requestAnimationFrame(animate);
    composer.render(); // Render using the composer
}
animate();
```

Motion Blur Effect

Motion blur simulates the blurring of objects in motion, enhancing realism during fast movements.

1. **Add the Motion Blur Pass**:

```javascript
Copy code
const motionBlurPass = new THREE.MotionBlurPass();
composer.addPass(motionBlurPass);
```

Depth of Field Effect

Depth of field creates a focus effect, blurring parts of the scene that are not in focus.

1. **Add the Depth of Field Pass**:

```javascript
Copy code
const dofPass = new THREE.BokehPass(scene, camera, {
    focus: 1.0,
    aperture: 0.025,
    maxDepth: 2.0,
    minDepth: 0.0,
});
composer.addPass(dofPass);
```

Final Render Call

Ensure to call the composer's render method in your animation loop to apply all post-processing effects:

```javascript
Copy code
function animate() {
    requestAnimationFrame(animate);
    composer.render();
}
animate();
```

Implementing Particle Systems

Particle systems are essential for creating effects like smoke, fire, rain, and explosions. Three.js provides a straightforward way to implement particle systems.

Step 1: Setting Up the Particle System

1. **Create a Particle Geometry**: Use THREE.BufferGeometry to create the geometry for the particles.

```javascript
Copy code
const particleCount = 1000;
const particles = new THREE.BufferGeometry();
const positions = new Float32Array(particleCount * 3); // 3
components per vertex (x, y, z)

for (let i = 0; i < particleCount; i++) {
    positions[i * 3] = (Math.random() - 0.5) * 10; // x
```

```
    positions[i * 3 + 1] = (Math.random() - 0.5) * 10; // y
    positions[i * 3 + 2] = (Math.random() - 0.5) * 10; // z
}

particles.setAttribute('position', new
THREE.BufferAttribute(positions, 3));
```

Step 2: Creating a Particle Material

Next, create a material for the particles using THREE.PointsMaterial.

```javascript
Copy code
const particleMaterial = new THREE.PointsMaterial({ color:
0xffffff, size: 0.1 });
```

Step 3: Creating the Particle System

Combine the geometry and material into a THREE.Points object.

```javascript
Copy code
const particleSystem = new THREE.Points(particles,
particleMaterial);
scene.add(particleSystem);
```

Step 4: Animating the Particles

Finally, update the particles' positions in the animation loop to create a dynamic effect.

```javascript
Copy code
function animateParticles() {
    const positions =
    particleSystem.geometry.attributes.position.array;

    for (let i = 0; i < particleCount; i++) {
        positions[i * 3 + 1] -= 0.01; // Move particles down
        if (positions[i * 3 + 1] < -5) {
            positions[i * 3 + 1] = 5; // Reset particle position
        }
    }

    particleSystem.geometry.attributes.position.needsUpdate =
    true; // Update the geometry
}

function animate() {
    requestAnimationFrame(animate);
    animateParticles(); // Update particle positions
    composer.render(); // Render the scene with post-processing
}
animate();
```

In this chapter, we explored the intricate world of advanced materials and shaders in Three.js. Understanding shaders, particularly GLSL, allows developers to create stunning visual effects that enhance the overall quality of 3D games. By learning how to implement custom shaders, apply post-processing effects, and create particle systems, you are now equipped with essential skills to elevate your game's visual fidelity.

As you continue to experiment with shaders and materials, remember that the only limit is your creativity. The techniques and concepts covered in this chapter will enable you to push the boundaries of what is possible in 3D game development, creating immersive experiences that captivate players and keep them coming back for more.

Chapter 12: Working with Sound and Music

S ound and music play a crucial role in enhancing the immersive experience of a game. They can set the mood, signal important events, and provide feedback to players. In this chapter, we will explore how to incorporate sound and music into your 3D games using JavaScript, focusing on adding background music and sound effects, leveraging the Web Audio API, triggering sounds based on events, and implementing 3D positional audio. By the end of this chapter, you'll have a solid understanding of how to enhance your game with sound, creating a more engaging experience for players.

Adding Background Music and Sound Effects

Background Music

Background music helps create the atmosphere of a game. It can evoke emotions, build tension, or provide a sense of adventure. Here's how to add background music to your Three.js game:

1. **Prepare Your Audio Files**: Ensure your music is in a web-friendly format such as MP3 or OGG. For best compatibility across browsers, consider providing multiple formats.
2. **Using the Audio Loader**: Three.js provides an AudioLoader that makes

it easy to load and play audio files. Here's how to implement it:

```javascript
Copy code
const listener = new THREE.AudioListener();
camera.add(listener); // Attach the listener to the camera

const backgroundMusic = new THREE.Audio(listener);
const audioLoader = new THREE.AudioLoader();

audioLoader.load('path/to/your/music.mp3', (buffer) => {
    backgroundMusic.setBuffer(buffer);
    backgroundMusic.setLoop(true); // Loop the music
    backgroundMusic.setVolume(0.5); // Set volume (0.0 to 1.0)
    backgroundMusic.play(); // Start playing the music
});
```

Sound Effects

Sound effects provide immediate feedback to players during gameplay, enhancing their experience. Similar to background music, you can use the AudioLoader to load sound effects.

1. **Load and Play Sound Effects**:

```javascript
Copy code
const soundEffect = new THREE.Audio(listener);
audioLoader.load('path/to/your/soundeffect.mp3', (buffer) => {
    soundEffect.setBuffer(buffer);
    soundEffect.setVolume(1.0); // Set volume for the sound effect
});

// Function to trigger the sound effect
```

```
function playSoundEffect() {
    soundEffect.play();
}
```

1. **Triggering Sound Effects**: You can call the playSoundEffect() function based on specific events in your game, such as player actions or interactions with objects.

Working with the Web Audio API

While Three.js simplifies audio management, you may want to leverage the full capabilities of the Web Audio API for more advanced audio control. This API provides robust features for sound processing, playback, and manipulation.

Setting Up the Web Audio API

To begin using the Web Audio API, you need to create an audio context:

```javascript
Copy code
const audioContext = new (window.AudioContext ||
window.webkitAudioContext)();
```

Loading Audio Files

Instead of using THREE.AudioLoader, you can manually load audio files using the Web Audio API. Here's how:

```javascript
Copy code
```

```
function loadAudio(url) {
    return fetch(url)
        .then(response => response.arrayBuffer())
        .then(data => audioContext.decodeAudioData(data));
}

loadAudio('path/to/your/music.mp3').then((buffer) => {
    const source = audioContext.createBufferSource();
    source.buffer = buffer;
    source.connect(audioContext.destination);
    source.loop = true; // Loop the audio
    source.start(0); // Start playing the audio
});
```

Advanced Audio Features

The Web Audio API provides various advanced features, such as:

- **Gain Nodes**: To control the volume of the audio.

```javascript
Copy code
const gainNode = audioContext.createGain();
gainNode.gain.setValueAtTime(0.5, audioContext.currentTime); //
Set volume
source.connect(gainNode);
gainNode.connect(audioContext.destination);
```

- **Panner Nodes**: To create 3D sound effects, allowing audio to come from different positions in your scene.

```javascript
Copy code
const panner = audioContext.createPanner();
panner.setPosition(0, 0, 0); // Set the position of the sound
source.connect(panner);
panner.connect(audioContext.destination);
```

Triggering Sounds Based on Events

Triggering sounds in response to events in your game can significantly enhance player engagement. This section will cover how to trigger sounds based on various game events, such as player actions, collisions, or interactions with objects.

Example: Playing Sounds on User Input

Consider a scenario where you want to play a sound effect when a player clicks a button. Here's how to implement that:

1. **Add an Event Listener**:

```javascript
Copy code
const button = document.getElementById('play-sound-button');
button.addEventListener('click', () => {
    playSoundEffect();
});
```

Example: Playing Sounds on Object Interactions

In a game, you might want to trigger sounds when players interact with objects. For instance, when a player collects an item, you can play a sound effect.

1. **Collision Detection**: Implement a method to detect collisions with objects in your scene.

```javascript
Copy code
function checkCollision(player, item) {
    if (player.position.distanceTo(item.position) < 1.0) { //
    Check if close enough
        playSoundEffect(); // Play sound upon collection
        // Additional logic for collecting the item
    }
}
```

Example: Sound Effects for Game Events

You can also trigger sounds based on game states, such as starting or ending a game.

1. **Game State Management**:

```javascript
Copy code
let isGameRunning = false;

function startGame() {
    isGameRunning = true;
```

```
    backgroundMusic.play(); // Play background music when game
    starts
}

function endGame() {
    isGameRunning = false;
    backgroundMusic.stop(); // Stop music when game ends
    playSoundEffect(); // Play end game sound effect
}
```

Implementing 3D Positional Audio

3D positional audio enhances the realism of your game by making sounds appear to come from specific locations in the 3D space. This effect is achieved by simulating how sound travels and how it interacts with the environment.

Setting Up 3D Positional Audio

1. **Create an Audio Listener**: The audio listener represents the player's ears in the scene.

```
javascript
Copy code
const listener = new THREE.AudioListener();
camera.add(listener); // Attach listener to the camera
```

1. **Create a Positional Audio Source**: This audio source represents the sound emitting from a specific position in your scene.

```javascript
javascript
Copy code
const positionalSound = new THREE.PositionalAudio(listener);
const audioLoader = new THREE.AudioLoader();

audioLoader.load('path/to/your/soundeffect.mp3', (buffer) => {
    positionalSound.setBuffer(buffer);
    positionalSound.setRefDistance(20); // Distance at which the
    sound is at maximum volume
    positionalSound.setLoop(true);
});
```

Adding Positional Audio to Objects

You can attach the positional audio source to any object in your scene. For example, if you have a moving enemy, you can add sound to that enemy.

```javascript
javascript
Copy code
const enemy = new THREE.Mesh(geometry, material);
enemy.add(positionalSound); // Attach positional audio to the enemy
scene.add(enemy);

// Start playing the sound
positionalSound.play();
```

Adjusting Positional Audio Properties

You can fine-tune various properties of the positional audio to achieve the desired effect:

- **Reference Distance**: Controls the distance at which the sound is perceived at full volume.

```javascript
Copy code
positionalSound.setRefDistance(10);
```

- **Max Distance**: The maximum distance at which the sound can be heard.

```javascript
Copy code
positionalSound.setMaxDistance(50);
```

- **Roll-off Factor**: Determines how quickly the sound fades as the listener moves away from the source.

```javascript
Copy code
positionalSound.setRolloffFactor(2);
```

Simulating 3D Audio in the Scene

To see how 3D positional audio works, consider a scenario where the player moves through a space filled with sounds emanating from various objects. As the player gets closer to these objects, the sounds should become louder, while they fade as the player moves away.

1. **Update Audio Positions**: In your animation loop, you might want to update the positions of the audio sources based on the game state.

```javascript
Copy code
function animate() {
    requestAnimationFrame(animate);

    // Update positional sound based on object movement
    positionalSound.position.copy(enemy.position);

    composer.render(); // Render the scene
}
animate();
```

Best Practices for Working with Sound in Games

Use High-Quality Audio Files

Always use high-quality audio files to ensure the best audio experience for your players. Poor audio quality can detract from even the most visually stunning games.

Optimize Audio Loading

Loading large audio files can slow down the game's initial loading time. Consider using techniques such as preloading, lazy loading, or compressing audio files to improve performance.

Control Volume and Balance

Provide options for players to adjust the volume of music and sound effects independently. This allows players to customize their audio experience according to their preferences.

Keep Audio Feedback Clear

Ensure that sound effects provide clear feedback to players. Sounds should be distinct and easily associated with specific actions or events in the game.

Test on Multiple Devices

Audio can behave differently on various devices and browsers. Always test your game on multiple platforms to ensure consistent audio performance.

In this chapter, we explored the vital role of sound and music in enhancing the immersive experience of 3D games. By adding background music and sound effects, utilizing the Web Audio API, and implementing 3D positional audio, you can create a rich auditory environment that captivates players.

As you continue to develop your 3D game, remember that sound is not just an afterthought; it's an essential component that can significantly impact the overall player experience. By applying the concepts and techniques covered in this chapter, you are now equipped to create an engaging and immersive audio experience for your game, enriching the gameplay and leaving a lasting impression on your players.

Chapter 13: Optimizing Game Performance

O
ptimizing performance is a crucial aspect of game development, particularly in 3D game development, where resources are limited and performance demands are high. In this chapter, we will explore various techniques and strategies to optimize your 3D games using JavaScript and Three.js. We'll cover reducing model complexity and draw calls, implementing Level of Detail (LOD) techniques, optimizing textures and materials, and understanding memory management and garbage collection. By the end of this chapter, you will have a solid foundation in performance optimization that will help your game run smoothly across a range of devices.

Reducing Model Complexity and Draw Calls

Understanding Model Complexity

Model complexity refers to the number of vertices, edges, and faces that make up a 3D model. Higher complexity typically leads to increased computational requirements, which can slow down rendering performance. Here are some strategies to reduce model complexity:

1. **Simplify Geometry**: Use lower-polygon models where higher detail is not necessary. This can significantly reduce the load on the GPU. For instance, consider using box models for distant objects instead of

detailed meshes.

2. **Combine Geometries**: If your scene contains many small objects, consider combining them into a single geometry. This reduces the number of draw calls, as the GPU can render them all at once.

```javascript
Copy code
const mergedGeometry =
THREE.BufferGeometryUtils.mergeBufferGeometries([geometry1,
geometry2]);
const mesh = new THREE.Mesh(mergedGeometry, material);
scene.add(mesh);
```

1. **Use Instancing**: For repeated objects (like trees in a forest or rocks in a landscape), use instancing. Instanced meshes allow you to render multiple copies of the same geometry efficiently.

```javascript
Copy code
const instancedMesh = new THREE.InstancedMesh(geometry, material,
count);
for (let i = 0; i < count; i++) {
    const matrix = new THREE.Matrix4();
    matrix.setPosition(Math.random() * 10, 0, Math.random() * 10);
    instancedMesh.setMatrixAt(i, matrix);
}
scene.add(instancedMesh);
```

Reducing Draw Calls

A draw call occurs when the GPU is instructed to render an object. Each draw call has overhead, so reducing the number of draw calls can greatly enhance performance. Here are some tips:

1. **Batching Draw Calls**: Grouping similar objects together can reduce the number of draw calls. For example, you can batch together all objects that share the same material.
2. **Use Texture Atlases**: Combine multiple textures into a single texture atlas. This allows you to map different parts of the atlas to different objects, minimizing the number of material switches.

```javascript
Copy code
const textureAtlas = new
THREE.TextureLoader().load('path/to/atlas.png');
const material = new THREE.MeshBasicMaterial({ map: textureAtlas
});
```

1. **Use Frustum Culling**: Implement frustum culling to avoid rendering objects that are not visible to the camera. Three.js does this automatically for mesh objects, but ensure that your models are appropriately set up with bounding boxes.

Level of Detail (LOD) Techniques

Level of Detail (LOD) is a rendering optimization technique that improves performance by using different levels of detail for objects based on their distance from the camera. The further an object is from the camera, the less detail is needed to render it.

Implementing LOD

1. **Create Multiple LOD Models**: Prepare several versions of your model at different resolutions (high, medium, and low).
2. **Using the THREE.LOD Class**:

```javascript
Copy code
const lod = new THREE.LOD();

const highResMesh = new THREE.Mesh(highResGeometry, material);
const mediumResMesh = new THREE.Mesh(mediumResGeometry, material);
const lowResMesh = new THREE.Mesh(lowResGeometry, material);

lod.addLevel(highResMesh, 0);    // Add high resolution for close
distance
lod.addLevel(mediumResMesh, 50); // Add medium resolution for
medium distance
lod.addLevel(lowResMesh, 100);   // Add low resolution for far
distance

scene.add(lod);
```

1. **Automatic LOD Switching**: Three.js automatically switches between LOD levels based on the camera distance. This helps ensure that only the necessary detail is rendered.

Benefits of LOD

Using LOD can significantly enhance performance, especially in scenes with many objects. By displaying lower-detail models for distant objects, you reduce the number of vertices processed by the GPU, allowing for smoother rendering and improved frame rates.

Optimizing Textures and Materials

Textures and materials are integral to the visual quality of your game but can also be significant performance bottlenecks. Optimizing these elements is essential for ensuring your game runs efficiently.

Texture Optimization Techniques

1. **Texture Size**: Reduce the dimensions of your textures. Higher resolution textures consume more memory and require more processing power to render. A common practice is to use 512x512 or 1024x1024 textures for most game objects.
2. **Use Compressed Textures**: Utilize texture compression formats like DDS, PVR, or ASTC. Compressed textures can significantly reduce memory usage and improve loading times.
3. **Mipmap Generation**: Use mipmaps for your textures. Mipmaps are pre-calculated, downscaled versions of your texture that improve rendering performance and reduce artifacts when textures are viewed at a distance.

```javascript
Copy code
const textureLoader = new THREE.TextureLoader();
const texture = textureLoader.load('path/to/texture.jpg',
(texture) => {
    texture.generateMipmaps = true; // Enable mipmaps
    texture.minFilter = THREE.LinearMipMapLinearFilter; // Set
    mipmap filtering
});
```

1. **Texture Atlases**: As mentioned earlier, combining multiple textures into a single atlas can reduce the number of texture bindings required during rendering, improving performance.

Material Optimization Techniques

1. **Use Fewer Material Types**: Limit the number of different materials in your scene. Each material requires its own shader, which adds overhead. By using a few materials across multiple objects, you can minimize the impact on performance.
2. **Optimize Shader Complexity**: The complexity of your shaders can significantly impact performance. Avoid unnecessary calculations in your shaders, and use simpler shaders for objects that do not require advanced effects.
3. **Avoid Transparency**: Transparent materials can complicate rendering and sorting. Where possible, use opaque materials, and consider using alpha testing instead of blending.
4. **Use Basic Materials for Non-Interactive Objects**: For objects that do not need complex interactions or shading (like background elements), use simpler materials such as MeshBasicMaterial.

Memory Management and Garbage Collection

Efficient memory management is essential for maintaining optimal performance in your game. Poor memory management can lead to performance degradation, crashes, and a poor user experience.

Understanding Memory Management

1. **Memory Allocation**: As you create objects in your game, they consume memory. Monitor how much memory your application is using and aim to minimize memory usage where possible.
2. **Garbage Collection**: JavaScript uses automatic garbage collection to free up memory that is no longer needed. However, you can help the garbage collector by nullifying references to objects you no longer need.

```javascript
Copy code
function removeObject(object) {
    scene.remove(object); // Remove from scene
    object.geometry.dispose(); // Dispose geometry
    object.material.dispose(); // Dispose material
    object = null; // Nullify reference
}
```

Memory Management Strategies

1. **Pooling Objects**: Instead of creating and destroying objects repeatedly (which can be expensive), consider implementing an object pooling system. Create a pool of reusable objects that can be enabled or disabled as needed.

```javascript
Copy code
const pool = [];
function getObjectFromPool() {
    if (pool.length > 0) {
        return pool.pop(); // Reuse an object from the pool
    }
    return new THREE.Mesh(geometry, material); // Create a new
    object if pool is empty
}

function returnObjectToPool(object) {
    pool.push(object); // Return object to pool for reuse
}
```

1. **Monitor Memory Usage**: Use browser developer tools to monitor memory usage and detect memory leaks. Look for objects that remain in memory after they should have been garbage collected.

2. **Dispose of Unused Resources**: When an object is no longer needed, dispose of its resources (geometry, materials, textures) to free up memory.

3. **Limit Event Listeners**: Remove event listeners for objects that are no longer in use. Event listeners can create references that prevent garbage collection.

```javascript
Copy code
object.removeEventListener('click', onClick);
```

1. **Manage Animation Frames**: If you are using animation loops, ensure you clear references to objects that are no longer needed within those loops. For example, cancel any ongoing animations when the associated object is removed from the scene.

Optimizing game performance is a critical aspect of 3D game development. In this chapter, we covered essential techniques for reducing model complexity and draw calls, implementing Level of Detail (LOD) techniques, optimizing textures and materials, and managing memory effectively. By applying these strategies, you can enhance the performance of your game, ensuring smooth gameplay and an engaging experience for your players.

As you continue your journey in 3D game development, remember that optimization is an ongoing process. Regularly assess your game's performance and seek out new opportunities for improvement. With careful attention to optimization, you can create a visually stunning and highly performant game that players will love.

Chapter 14: Multiplayer Game Development

In today's gaming landscape, multiplayer experiences are often a defining feature of success. Whether players are teaming up to conquer challenges or competing for supremacy, creating a robust multiplayer environment can significantly enhance user engagement and enjoyment. In this chapter, we will delve into the key aspects of multiplayer game development using JavaScript and Three.js. We'll cover an introduction to WebSockets, techniques for synchronizing game state between clients, managing latency and lag compensation, and step-by-step guidance to build a simple multiplayer game.

Introduction to WebSockets

Understanding WebSockets

WebSockets provide a full-duplex communication channel over a single, long-lived connection. Unlike traditional HTTP requests, which are stateless and require new connections for each request, WebSockets enable real-time communication, making them ideal for multiplayer games. With WebSockets, the server and clients can send messages to each other independently and instantly, allowing for responsive gameplay experiences.

Benefits of Using WebSockets for Multiplayer Games

1. **Real-Time Communication**: WebSockets enable near-instantaneous data transfer, which is essential for maintaining game state and ensuring that players can interact with each other seamlessly.
2. **Reduced Overhead**: By maintaining a single open connection, WebSockets reduce the overhead associated with establishing multiple connections, making them more efficient for data transmission.
3. **Bidirectional Communication**: Both the server and clients can send messages to each other without waiting for a request, facilitating dynamic game interactions.

Setting Up a WebSocket Server

To implement WebSockets in your multiplayer game, you'll need a server to handle connections. Below is an example of setting up a simple WebSocket server using Node.js and the ws library.

1. **Install the ws library**:

```bash
Copy code
npm install ws
```

1. **Create a WebSocket server**:

```javascript
Copy code
const WebSocket = require('ws');
```

```javascript
const server = new WebSocket.Server({ port: 8080 });

server.on('connection', (socket) => {
    console.log('New client connected');

    socket.on('message', (message) => {
        console.log(`Received message: ${message}`);
        // Broadcast the message to all connected clients
        server.clients.forEach((client) => {
            if (client !== socket && client.readyState ===
            WebSocket.OPEN) {
                client.send(message);
            }
        });
    });

    socket.on('close', () => {
        console.log('Client disconnected');
    });
});

console.log('WebSocket server is running on ws://localhost:8080');
```

With this server, clients can connect, send messages, and receive messages from other clients, forming the basis for multiplayer interactions.

Synchronizing Game State Between Clients

The Importance of Game State Synchronization

In multiplayer games, it is crucial to keep all clients in sync regarding the game state. This includes player positions, scores, game events, and any other relevant data. Synchronization ensures that all players see the same game world and experience consistent interactions.

Strategies for Synchronizing Game State

1. **State Updates**: Regularly send state updates from the server to all connected clients. This can be done at a fixed interval or triggered by specific game events.

```javascript
Copy code
function broadcastGameState() {
    const gameState = { players, objects }; // Prepare game state
    data
    server.clients.forEach((client) => {
        if (client.readyState === WebSocket.OPEN) {
            client.send(JSON.stringify(gameState));
        }
    });
}

setInterval(broadcastGameState, 100); // Broadcast game state
every 100 ms
```

1. **Event-Based Synchronization**: Instead of continuously sending the entire game state, consider sending updates only when specific events occur (e.g., player movement, object interaction).

```javascript
Copy code
socket.on('playerMove', (data) => {
    // Update player position on the server
    updatePlayerPosition(data.playerId, data.position);
    // Broadcast the player move event to other clients
    broadcastEvent('playerMoved', data);
});
```

1. **Client-Side Prediction**: To enhance responsiveness, implement client-side prediction. When a player takes an action (e.g., moves), the client can immediately update its game state while also sending the action to the server. This reduces perceived latency.

```javascript
Copy code
function movePlayer(playerId, newPosition) {
    // Update local player position
    players[playerId].position = newPosition;
    // Send move event to the server
    socket.send(JSON.stringify({ type: 'playerMove', playerId,
    position: newPosition }));
}
```

1. **Interpolation and Extrapolation**: To smooth out the movement of other players, use interpolation (for players already in motion) and extrapolation (for players whose state hasn't been updated yet).

- **Interpolation**: Gradually move the local player towards the last known position of the remote player.
- **Extrapolation**: Predict where the remote player will be based on their last known velocity.

Handling Latency and Lag Compensation

Understanding Latency

Latency refers to the delay between a player's action and the response received from the server. In multiplayer games, high latency can lead to a poor player experience, causing actions to feel unresponsive and disjointed.

Techniques for Handling Latency

1. **Lag Compensation Techniques**: To ensure a fair experience, implement lag compensation techniques, such as rewinding the game state on the server when processing player actions. This allows the server to simulate the game state as it was when the action was initiated.

```javascript
Copy code
function handlePlayerAction(action) {
    const currentTime = getCurrentTime();
    const playerTime = action.timestamp; // Time when the action
    was sent

    // Rewind game state to the time of the action
    const stateAtActionTime = getGameStateAtTime(playerTime);
    processAction(stateAtActionTime, action);
}
```

1. **Client-Side Lag Compensation**: On the client side, implement a "ghosting" mechanism to show the player's past actions. This can help visualize where players are compared to where they appear on the server.
2. **Adjustable Interpolation**: Adjust the interpolation delay based on the player's ping to the server. Players with lower latency can receive more immediate feedback, while players with higher latency can see smoother transitions.
3. **Server-Side Prediction**: In addition to client-side prediction, you can implement server-side prediction to correct discrepancies between client states. The server can adjust the position based on the player's last known velocity and actions.

131

Measuring Latency

To effectively manage latency, monitor the round-trip time (RTT) between clients and the server. This information can be used to adjust rendering and input responses.

```javascript
Copy code
const ping = setInterval(() => {
    const startTime = Date.now();
    socket.send(JSON.stringify({ type: 'ping' }));
    socket.onmessage = (message) => {
        const latency = Date.now() - startTime;
        console.log(`Ping: ${latency} ms`);
    };
}, 1000);
```

Building a Simple Multiplayer Game

Game Concept

For our example, we will create a simple multiplayer game where players can move around a 2D space and interact with each other. Players will be represented by colored circles, and they will be able to move using the keyboard.

Setting Up the Game

1. **Create the Game Client**:

```html
Copy code
```

```
<html>
<head>
    <title>Multiplayer Game</title>
    <style>
        canvas { border: 1px solid black; }
    </style>
</head>
<body>
    <canvas id="gameCanvas" width="800" height="600"></canvas>
    <script src="https://threejs.org/build/three.min.js"></script>
    <script>
        const canvas = document.getElementById('gameCanvas');
        const ctx = canvas.getContext('2d');
        const socket = new WebSocket('ws://localhost:8080');

        const players = {};

        socket.onmessage = (event) => {
            const data = JSON.parse(event.data);
            if (data.type === 'playerMoved') {
                players[data.playerId] = data.position; // Update
                player position
            }
        };

        function render() {
            ctx.clearRect(0, 0, canvas.width, canvas.height);
            for (const playerId in players) {
                const { x, y } = players[playerId];
                ctx.beginPath();
                ctx.arc(x, y, 10, 0, Math.PI * 2);
                ctx.fillStyle = 'blue'; // Color of the player
                ctx.fill();
            }
            requestAnimationFrame(render);
        }
        render();

        document.addEventListener('keydown', (event) => {
            const playerId = 'yourPlayerId'; // Unique player ID
```

```
            let newPosition;
            switch (event.key) {
                case 'ArrowUp':
                    newPosition = { x: players[playerId].x, y:
                    players[playerId].y - 5 };
                    break;
                case 'ArrowDown':
                    newPosition = { x: players[playerId].x, y:
                    players[playerId].y + 5 };
                    break;
                case 'ArrowLeft':
                    newPosition = { x: players[playerId].x - 5, y:
                    players[playerId].y };
                    break;
                case 'ArrowRight':
                    newPosition = { x: players[playerId].x + 5, y:
                    players[playerId].y };
                    break;
                default:
                    return;
            }
            players[playerId] = newPosition;
            socket.send(JSON.stringify({ type: 'playerMove',
            playerId, position: newPosition }));
        });
    </script>
</body>
</html>
```

Server Logic

In the previously established WebSocket server, include logic to handle player movements and broadcast them to other clients. Here's how to update the server:

1. **Add Player Management**:

```javascript
Copy code
const players = {};

server.on('connection', (socket) => {
    const playerId = generateUniqueId();
    players[playerId] = { x: 0, y: 0 }; // Initial position

    socket.on('message', (message) => {
        const data = JSON.parse(message);
        if (data.type === 'playerMove') {
            players[data.playerId] = data.position; // Update
            player position
            broadcastEvent('playerMoved', { playerId:
            data.playerId, position: data.position });
        }
    });
});

function broadcastEvent(type, data) {
    const event = JSON.stringify({ type, ...data });
    server.clients.forEach((client) => {
        if (client.readyState === WebSocket.OPEN) {
            client.send(event);
        }
    });
}
```

Testing the Game

1. Run the WebSocket server using Node.js.
2. Open multiple browser tabs to simulate different players.
3. Use the arrow keys to move your player around the canvas.

With this setup, you should have a basic multiplayer game where players can move around and see each other's movements in real-time.

Enhancements

To enhance this basic multiplayer game, consider implementing the following features:

1. **Player Colors**: Assign different colors to each player for better identification.
2. **Game Lobby**: Implement a lobby system for players to join before starting the game.
3. **Game Events**: Add game events, such as collecting items or achieving goals.
4. **Chat System**: Implement a chat system to facilitate communication between players.
5. **Mobile Compatibility**: Ensure the game is responsive and works well on mobile devices.

In this chapter, we explored the essential components of multiplayer game development using JavaScript and WebSockets. We discussed the significance of real-time communication, strategies for synchronizing game states, and techniques for managing latency and lag compensation. By building a simple multiplayer game, we demonstrated the practical application of these concepts. As you continue to develop your multiplayer game, consider the features and enhancements that can elevate the player experience, fostering an engaging and interactive environment. Happy coding!

Chapter 15: Debugging and Testing Your Game

D
ebugging and testing are crucial phases in the game development process, particularly for multiplayer 3D games where multiple players interact in real time. This chapter will cover essential debugging tools for JavaScript and Three.js, performance profiling techniques, testing game logic and physics, and strategies for cross-browser testing and ensuring compatibility. By understanding these aspects, you can enhance your game's stability, performance, and overall user experience.

Debugging Tools for JavaScript and Three.js

1. Console Debugging

One of the most fundamental methods for debugging JavaScript is the use of the console. The console provides real-time feedback about errors and logs messages that can help track down issues in your code.

Using console.log()

You can insert console.log() statements throughout your code to check the flow of execution and the values of variables at different points in time.

```
javascript
Copy code
```

```
console.log('Player position:', player.position);
```

This line logs the player's position, allowing you to verify that the coordinates are updated correctly during gameplay.

Error Logging

JavaScript errors are logged automatically in the console. You can view error messages and stack traces to pinpoint the line of code that caused the issue.

2. Browser Developer Tools

All modern web browsers come equipped with developer tools that provide an extensive suite of debugging features.

Inspecting Elements

The Elements tab in the Developer Tools allows you to inspect the HTML structure of your game, including the canvas. This is particularly useful for verifying that the DOM is rendered correctly.

Network Monitoring

The Network tab helps track all network requests made by your game, such as loading assets or WebSocket connections. You can view the status of each request and check for any errors.

JavaScript Debugger

The Sources tab provides a built-in JavaScript debugger that lets you set breakpoints, step through your code, and inspect variable values at runtime.

- **Setting Breakpoints**: Click on the line number in the Sources tab to set a breakpoint. When the code execution reaches that line, it will pause, allowing you to inspect the current state of the application.
- **Stepping Through Code**: Use the Step Over, Step Into, and Step Out options to navigate through your code line by line or to jump into function calls.

3. Three.js Inspector

The Three.js Inspector is a useful tool for debugging Three.js applications. It allows you to visualize your 3D scene in real-time, inspect objects, and modify their properties.

- **Viewing Scene Graph**: The inspector provides a visual representation of your scene graph, allowing you to see all objects in your scene, their hierarchy, and properties.
- **Modifying Object Properties**: You can change object properties (such as position, rotation, and material) in real-time and see the results immediately.

4. Error Handling in WebSocket Connections

When developing multiplayer games, handling WebSocket errors is crucial. Use the onerror event handler to capture and log errors related to your WebSocket connections.

```javascript
Copy code
socket.onerror = (event) => {
    console.error('WebSocket error:', event);
};
```

This will help you diagnose issues related to network connectivity or server errors.

Performance Profiling

Performance profiling is vital for ensuring that your game runs smoothly, especially when rendering complex 3D scenes or handling multiple player interactions. Here are some tools and techniques for profiling performance.

1. Chrome Performance Tab

The Performance tab in Chrome Developer Tools allows you to record the performance of your application and analyze various metrics.

- **Recording Performance**: Click the Record button, perform actions in your game, and then stop recording. This will provide a detailed breakdown of CPU usage, frames per second (FPS), and rendering times.
- **Analyzing the Timeline**: The timeline shows how much time is spent on rendering, scripting, and painting. Look for long bars in the rendering phase, as these indicate bottlenecks that need optimization.

2. FPS Counter

Integrating a simple FPS counter into your game can help you monitor performance in real-time. Here's a basic example using Three.js:

```javascript
Copy code
let fps = 0;
const clock = new THREE.Clock();

function render() {
    fps++;
    const delta = clock.getDelta();

    // Update your game state and render the scene
    requestAnimationFrame(render);

    // Display the FPS counter
    if (delta >= 1) {
        console.log(`FPS: ${fps}`);
        fps = 0; // Reset FPS counter
    }
}
```

3. Identifying Performance Bottlenecks

1. **Profile Render Calls**: Check how many draw calls are being made each frame. Too many draw calls can degrade performance. Combine geometries or use texture atlases to minimize draw calls.
2. **Reduce Polygon Count**: High polygon counts can slow rendering. Use level of detail (LOD) techniques to load lower-polygon models for distant objects.
3. **Optimize Textures**: Large texture sizes can impact performance. Use compressed textures where possible and ensure they're appropriately sized for their use case.

4. Memory Profiling

Memory leaks can significantly affect game performance. Use the Memory tab in Chrome Developer Tools to track memory usage.

- **Heap Snapshot**: Take heap snapshots to identify memory usage over time. Compare snapshots to detect memory leaks.
- **Garbage Collection**: Monitor how frequently garbage collection occurs and ensure that you're properly disposing of objects that are no longer needed in your game.

Testing Game Logic and Physics

Testing your game logic and physics is essential for ensuring a smooth gameplay experience. Below are strategies for effectively testing your game.

1. Unit Testing

Unit testing involves testing individual functions or components of your game for correctness. Using a testing framework like Jest or Mocha, you can write tests to verify that your functions behave as expected.

Example of a Simple Unit Test with Jest

```javascript
Copy code
// player.js
export function movePlayer(player, direction) {
    switch (direction) {
        case 'up':
            player.y += 1;
            break;
        case 'down':
            player.y -= 1;
            break;
        case 'left':
            player.x -= 1;
            break;
        case 'right':
            player.x += 1;
            break;
    }
    return player;
}

// player.test.js
import { movePlayer } from './player';

test('moves player up', () => {
    const player = { x: 0, y: 0 };
    const newPlayer = movePlayer(player, 'up');
    expect(newPlayer.y).toBe(1);
});
```

2. Integration Testing

Integration testing focuses on testing how different components of your game work together. For example, you might want to ensure that player movements update the game state correctly and that collisions are detected as expected.

3. Physics Testing

Testing your physics engine involves verifying that the physics interactions in your game behave as intended.

1. **Collision Detection**: Test various scenarios where collisions should occur. Ensure that objects collide and respond appropriately.
2. **Gravity and Forces**: Simulate various forces and check that objects fall or move as expected when subjected to gravity or other forces.
3. **Performance Under Load**: Test your game with multiple objects and players interacting simultaneously to ensure that the physics engine can handle the load without performance degradation.

Cross-Browser Testing and Compatibility

With players accessing games from various browsers and devices, ensuring cross-browser compatibility is essential. Below are strategies for effective cross-browser testing.

1. Browser Compatibility Testing

- **Testing in Multiple Browsers**: Regularly test your game in different browsers (Chrome, Firefox, Safari, Edge) to ensure consistent behavior. Each browser may render and execute JavaScript differently.
- **Responsive Design**: Ensure that your game is responsive and looks good on various screen sizes and devices. Use CSS media queries and flexible layouts to achieve this.

2. Using Browser Testing Tools

Several tools can help automate cross-browser testing:

1. **BrowserStack**: A cloud-based platform that allows you to test your

application across various browsers and devices.

2. **CrossBrowserTesting**: Similar to BrowserStack, it provides a wide range of browser and device combinations for testing.

3. **Selenium**: An open-source testing framework that allows for automated testing of web applications across different browsers.

3. Polyfills and Shims

To ensure compatibility with older browsers, you may need to use polyfills or shims for features that are not natively supported. Libraries like core-js can help add support for newer JavaScript features.

```javascript
Copy code
import 'core-js/features/promise'; // Polyfill for Promises
```

4. Feature Detection

Instead of relying on user-agent detection, use feature detection to ensure that the required functionalities are available in the user's browser.

```javascript
Copy code
if ('WebGLRenderingContext' in window) {
    // WebGL is supported
} else {
    alert('Your browser does not support WebGL. Please update or
    switch to a modern browser.');
}
```

Debugging and testing are critical aspects of game development that can significantly impact the player experience. By utilizing various debugging tools, performance profiling techniques, testing game logic and physics, and ensuring cross-browser compatibility, you can create a more robust and enjoyable game. As you refine your multiplayer 3D game, consider the importance of thorough testing and debugging practices to deliver a polished final product.

Chapter 16: Deploying Your Game

Deploying your 3D game is a crucial step that brings your project to life, allowing players to experience your hard work. This chapter will guide you through the process of packaging your game for the web, exploring hosting options, implementing version control with Git, and utilizing continuous integration and deployment (CI/CD) to streamline your workflow.

Packaging Your Game for the Web

Packaging your game involves preparing all the necessary files and assets so that they can be served efficiently to users. Here's how to do it effectively.

1. File Structure

A well-organized file structure is key to making deployment easier and ensuring your game runs smoothly. A typical structure might look like this:

```bash
Copy code
/my-game          ├──────

  /assets         ├────
    /models       ├────
    /textures     └────
```

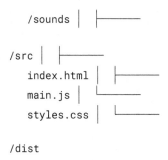

```
   /sounds  |  |————————
 /src  |  |————————
    index.html  |  |————————
    main.js  |  |————————
    styles.css  |  |————————

 /dist
```

- **assets/**: Contains all the game assets like 3D models, textures, and sound files.
- **src/**: Holds the source code, including HTML, CSS, and JavaScript files.
- **dist/**: A directory where you will output your packaged game files, typically optimized for production.

2. Bundling Your Code

To prepare your game for deployment, you often need to bundle your JavaScript code and other assets. Tools like Webpack, Parcel, or Rollup can help with this process.

Setting Up Webpack

1. **Install Webpack**:

```bash
Copy code
npm install --save-dev webpack webpack-cli
```

1. **Create a webpack.config.js file** in your project root:

```javascript
Copy code
const path = require('path');

module.exports = {
    entry: './src/main.js',
    output: {
        filename: 'bundle.js',
        path: path.resolve(__dirname, 'dist')
    },
    module: {
        rules: [
            {
                test: /\.js$/,
                exclude: /node_modules/,
                use: {
                    loader: 'babel-loader',
                    options: {
                        presets: ['@babel/preset-env']
                    }
                }
            }
        ]
    },
    mode: 'production'
};
```

1. **Bundle Your Code**: Run the following command to bundle your code:

```bash
Copy code
npx webpack
```

After running this command, you'll find a bundle.js file in the dist/ directory, ready for deployment.

3. Minification and Optimization

Minification reduces the size of your JavaScript, CSS, and HTML files, which is essential for faster load times. Many bundlers automatically minify your code in production mode.

- **CSS Minification**: Use tools like cssnano or integrate CSS minification in Webpack with mini-css-extract-plugin.
- **Image Optimization**: Use tools like ImageOptim or TinyPNG to compress image assets before deploying them.

4. Creating an index.html File

Your index.html file will serve as the entry point for your game. Ensure it links to your bundled JavaScript and includes necessary meta tags for better performance and compatibility.

```html
Copy code
<!DOCTYPE html>
<html lang="en">
<head>
    <meta charset="UTF-8">
    <meta name="viewport" content="width=device-width,
    initial-scale=1.0">
    <title>My 3D Game</title>
    <link rel="stylesheet" href="styles.css">
</head>
<body>
    <div id="game-container"></div>
    <script src="bundle.js"></script>
</body>
</html>
```

Hosting Options: Self-Hosting vs. Game Hosting Platforms

Once your game is packaged, it's time to decide where to host it. Here are two primary options: self-hosting and using game hosting platforms.

1. Self-Hosting

Self-hosting involves setting up your own server to serve your game. This gives you complete control but requires technical knowledge and maintenance.

Steps for Self-Hosting

1. **Choose a Web Server**: Popular options include Apache, Nginx, or Node.js.
2. **Set Up Your Server**: Follow the specific instructions for your chosen web server. For example, with Nginx, you would configure your nginx.conf file to point to your dist directory.
3. **Upload Your Files**: Use FTP, SFTP, or SSH to upload your files to the server.
4. **Domain Name**: Purchase a domain name and point it to your server's IP address.
5. **SSL Certificate**: Consider obtaining an SSL certificate for secure connections (HTTPS). Services like Let's Encrypt provide free SSL certificates.

2. Game Hosting Platforms

Game hosting platforms specialize in hosting games and often provide additional features like analytics, multiplayer support, and easier deployment options.

Popular Game Hosting Platforms

1. **Itch.io**: A popular platform for indie games, allowing you to upload

your game files and create a storefront.

2. **Game Jolt**: Similar to Itch.io, Game Jolt focuses on indie games, providing a community for developers and players.

3. **GitHub Pages**: If your game is a static web app, you can use GitHub Pages for free hosting. Simply push your code to a GitHub repository and enable GitHub Pages in the settings.

4. **Netlify or Vercel**: Both services offer free hosting with automatic deployment from Git repositories, making it easy to manage updates.

3. Cost Considerations

When choosing between self-hosting and game hosting platforms, consider the associated costs:

- **Self-Hosting**: Requires expenses for a domain, hosting service, and potentially server management.
- **Game Hosting Platforms**: Usually offer free tiers, but may take a percentage of sales if you sell your game.

Version Control with Git

Version control is essential for tracking changes, collaborating with others, and managing your game's development process.

1. Setting Up Git

1. **Initialize a Git Repository**: Navigate to your game's root directory and run:

```bash
Copy code
```

```
git init
```

1. **Create a .gitignore File**: This file specifies which files and directories should be ignored by Git. Common entries include:

```bash
Copy code
node_modules/
dist/
*.log
```

1. **Commit Your Changes**: Regularly commit your changes with descriptive messages.

```bash
Copy code
git add .
git commit -m "Initial commit"
```

2. Branching Strategy

Using branches allows you to work on features or fixes without affecting the main codebase.

- **Create a Branch**:

```bash
Copy code
```

```
git checkout -b feature/new-game-mode
```

- **Merge Changes**: Once your feature is complete and tested, merge it back into the main branch:

```
bash
Copy code
git checkout main
git merge feature/new-game-mode
```

3. Collaborating with Others

Git allows multiple developers to work on the same project simultaneously. Platforms like GitHub, GitLab, or Bitbucket provide remote repositories for collaboration.

- **Pull Requests**: Use pull requests to review code before merging changes. This helps maintain code quality and facilitates discussions.
- **Conflict Resolution**: Be prepared to resolve conflicts when multiple developers modify the same lines of code. Git provides tools to help manage these conflicts.

Continuous Integration and Deployment

Continuous integration (CI) and continuous deployment (CD) are practices that streamline the process of testing and deploying your game.

1. Setting Up CI/CD

1. **Choose a CI/CD Tool**: Popular options include GitHub Actions, Travis CI, CircleCI, and Jenkins.
2. **Create a Configuration File**: For example, with GitHub Actions, create a .github/workflows/main.yml file:

```yaml
Copy code
name: CI/CD

on:
  push:
    branches:
      - main

jobs:
  build:
    runs-on: ubuntu-latest
    steps:
    - name: Checkout code
      uses: actions/checkout@v2
    - name: Set up Node.js
      uses: actions/setup-node@v2
      with:
        node-version: '14'
    - name: Install dependencies
      run: npm install
    - name: Build the game
      run: npm run build
    - name: Deploy to GitHub Pages
      run: npm run deploy
```

2. Automated Testing

Integrate automated tests into your CI/CD pipeline to ensure code quality. Tools like Jest or Mocha can be used to write unit and integration tests.

3. Deployment Automation

Configure your CI/CD pipeline to automatically deploy your game to your hosting platform whenever changes are pushed to the main branch. This can save you time and reduce the risk of human error.

4. Monitoring and Feedback

After deployment, monitor your game's performance and gather user feedback. Tools like Google Analytics can help track user behavior and performance metrics, guiding future updates and improvements.

Deploying your 3D game is an exciting phase that involves packaging your game, choosing the right hosting options, implementing version control with Git, and utilizing continuous integration and deployment. By following best practices for deployment, you can ensure a smooth launch and provide players with an enjoyable gaming experience. As you continue to refine and expand your game, these deployment strategies will be invaluable in maintaining and improving your project. Happy deploying!

Chapter 17: Monetizing Your Game

In the competitive world of game development, creating a fantastic game is just the beginning. Once you've built your 3D game, the next crucial step is figuring out how to monetize it effectively. This chapter explores various monetization strategies, including in-game ads and purchases, paid game models, subscriptions, and donations, as well as marketing and promoting your game to reach a broader audience.

Adding In-Game Ads and Purchases

In-game advertising and purchases can provide a steady revenue stream, especially for free-to-play games. These methods allow players to enjoy your game without upfront costs while giving you the opportunity to earn money through ads and microtransactions.

1. In-Game Advertising

In-game advertising involves displaying ads during gameplay or on game menus. This can be an effective way to monetize your game without directly charging players.

Types of In-Game Ads

- **Banner Ads**: These are static or animated ads that appear at the top or bottom of the screen. They are less intrusive and can be effective for driving traffic to advertisers' websites.

- **Interstitial Ads**: Full-screen ads that appear at natural transition points in the game (like level changes) can be very engaging. However, they can also disrupt gameplay if overused.
- **Rewarded Ads**: Players watch a video ad in exchange for in-game rewards, such as extra lives or exclusive items. This type of ad often leads to higher engagement rates and positive player feedback.
- **Native Ads**: These ads blend seamlessly with the game's environment and do not disrupt gameplay. For example, a game might feature a branded vehicle or item that players can use.

Implementing In-Game Ads

To implement in-game ads, you can use ad networks like AdMob, Unity Ads, or Playwire. Here's a general process:

1. **Choose an Ad Network**: Select a network based on your target audience and game type. Research their SDKs and integration processes.
2. **Integrate the SDK**: Follow the documentation provided by the ad network to integrate their SDK into your game. This typically involves installing the SDK, initializing it, and adding code to display ads at appropriate times.
3. **Test Ads**: Before launching your game, test ads to ensure they display correctly and do not negatively impact the user experience.
4. **Monitor Performance**: Once your game is live, regularly check ad performance metrics provided by the ad network. Adjust your ad strategy based on player engagement and revenue data.

2. In-Game Purchases

In-game purchases (also known as microtransactions) allow players to buy virtual goods or currency within the game. This can enhance their experience while providing you with revenue.

Types of In-Game Purchases

- **Cosmetic Items**: These items do not affect gameplay but allow players to customize their avatars, weapons, or environments. Examples include skins, costumes, and emotes.
- **Power-Ups and Boosts**: Players can purchase items that enhance their gameplay, such as extra lives, energy boosts, or temporary invincibility. These items can make the game more enjoyable and engaging.
- **Game Currency**: Players can buy virtual currency used to purchase items within the game. This approach allows for a scalable pricing model, as you can offer various currency packages at different price points.
- **Expansion Packs**: Larger content updates, such as new levels, characters, or stories, can be sold as expansion packs. This can keep players engaged over a longer period.

Implementing In-Game Purchases

1. **Choose a Payment Provider**: Research and select a payment provider that suits your game's platform, such as Stripe, PayPal, or the app store's payment system (e.g., Google Play or Apple App Store).
2. **Set Up In-Game Store**: Create a user-friendly interface for players to browse and purchase items. Ensure that the store aligns with the game's aesthetics and is easy to navigate.
3. **Manage Transactions**: Implement server-side logic to handle transactions securely. Ensure that players receive their purchased items promptly.
4. **Analyze Sales Data**: Monitor in-game purchase data to understand player spending behavior. Use this information to optimize your offerings and marketing strategies.

Implementing a Paid Game Model

A paid game model requires players to purchase the game upfront, providing you with immediate revenue. While this model can be effective, it also requires careful planning and execution.

1. Pricing Your Game

Determining the right price for your game is critical. Consider the following factors:

- **Market Research**: Analyze similar games in your genre to see how they are priced. This can help you position your game competitively.
- **Game Quality**: Ensure that your game delivers a high-quality experience that justifies the price. Players are more likely to pay if they perceive value in your game.
- **Target Audience**: Understand your target audience's willingness to pay. Younger audiences or casual gamers may prefer lower prices, while dedicated gamers may be willing to pay more for a rich experience.

2. Offering Discounts and Promotions

Discounts and promotions can drive initial sales and boost visibility. Consider:

- **Launch Discounts**: Offer a limited-time discount during the launch to attract early adopters.
- **Seasonal Sales**: Participate in seasonal sales events (like Steam's Summer Sale) to increase visibility and encourage purchases.
- **Bundles**: Consider bundling your game with other titles or content to provide value and attract more buyers.

3. Pre-Orders and Early Access

Offering pre-orders or an early access version of your game can generate interest and revenue before the official launch.

- **Pre-Orders**: Allow players to purchase the game before it's released. This can help gauge interest and fund further development.

- **Early Access**: Release your game in a beta state, allowing players to purchase and play it while you continue to develop and improve it based on feedback.

Subscriptions and Donations

In addition to traditional monetization methods, consider subscription models and donations as alternative revenue streams.

1. Subscription Models

Subscription models involve players paying a recurring fee to access your game or its content. This model is particularly effective for games that receive regular updates or new content.

Types of Subscriptions

- **Monthly Subscriptions**: Players pay a fixed monthly fee for access to the game. This can work well for games with ongoing content updates.
- **Season Passes**: Offer a one-time purchase for access to exclusive content over a specific period, such as new levels, characters, or events.
- **Freemium Model**: Players can access basic gameplay for free but must subscribe to unlock additional content or features.

2. Implementing Subscriptions

1. **Choose a Subscription Platform**: Consider platforms like Patreon, Ko-fi, or your payment provider's subscription options.
2. **Create Tiered Subscription Plans**: Offer various subscription tiers with different benefits to appeal to a broader audience.
3. **Provide Exclusive Content**: Regularly release exclusive content for subscribers to maintain engagement and justify the subscription cost.
4. **Engage with Subscribers**: Build a community around your game through forums, social media, or Discord channels. Engage with your

subscribers to foster loyalty and encourage retention.

3. Donations

Donations can provide a supplemental income stream, especially for indie developers. You can set up donation options through platforms like PayPal or Buy Me a Coffee.

Strategies for Encouraging Donations

- **Transparency**: Let players know how their donations will support future development and improvements.
- **Incentives**: Offer incentives for donations, such as exclusive in-game items or recognition in the game credits.
- **Engagement**: Engage with your community and keep them updated on your game's progress. Building a strong relationship with players can encourage them to support you financially.

Marketing and Promoting Your Game

To successfully monetize your game, effective marketing and promotion are essential. Attracting players and building a community around your game can significantly enhance your revenue potential.

1. Building a Brand

Creating a strong brand identity for your game can help you stand out in a crowded market. Consider the following:

- **Logo and Visuals**: Design a memorable logo and consistent visual style that reflects your game's theme and tone.
- **Unique Selling Proposition (USP)**: Identify what makes your game unique compared to others. Highlight these features in your marketing materials.

- **Website**: Create a professional website for your game. Include information about the game, trailers, screenshots, and links to download or purchase it.

2. Creating a Marketing Plan

A well-thought-out marketing plan can guide your promotional efforts and maximize your reach.

Key Components of a Marketing Plan

- **Target Audience**: Define your target audience based on demographics, interests, and gaming preferences.
- **Marketing Channels**: Identify the most effective channels to reach your audience, such as social media, game forums, and influencers.
- **Content Strategy**: Develop a content strategy that includes blog posts, trailers, screenshots, and behind-the-scenes videos to engage your audience.
- **Budget**: Allocate a budget for marketing efforts, including paid advertising, influencer partnerships, and promotional events.

3. Utilizing Social Media

Social media platforms can be powerful tools for promoting your game and engaging with your audience.

Effective Social Media Strategies

- **Regular Updates**: Share regular updates on your game's development progress, including new features, gameplay mechanics, and behind-the-scenes content.
- **Engage with Your Audience**: Respond to comments, messages, and mentions. Building a community around your game can create loyal fans.
- **User-Generated Content**: Encourage players to share their experiences and content related to your game. Reposting user-generated content can

foster community engagement.

4. Collaborating with Influencers

Influencer marketing can help you reach a broader audience and build credibility.

Steps to Collaborate with Influencers

1. **Identify Relevant Influencers**: Research and identify influencers in the gaming community who align with your target audience.
2. **Reach Out**: Contact influencers with a personalized message introducing your game and proposing a collaboration.
3. **Provide Access**: Offer influencers access to your game for reviews, gameplay videos, or live streams. This exposure can attract new players and generate interest.
4. **Monitor Results**: Track the performance of influencer campaigns to assess their effectiveness. Adjust your strategy based on engagement and conversion rates.

5. Leveraging Game Communities

Engaging with gaming communities can significantly enhance your game's visibility and credibility.

Effective Community Engagement

- **Game Forums**: Participate in forums and discussions related to your game genre. Share insights, answer questions, and promote your game without being overly promotional.
- **Beta Testing**: Involve community members in beta testing. This not only generates interest but also provides valuable feedback for improvement.
- **Events and Competitions**: Organize events, contests, or challenges within your game community to foster engagement and excitement.

Conclusion

Monetizing your game requires a strategic approach that combines effective monetization methods with robust marketing efforts. By understanding your target audience and implementing the right strategies, you can maximize your game's revenue potential while providing players with an enjoyable experience. Whether through in-game ads, paid models, subscriptions, or community engagement, successful monetization is about creating value for both you and your players.

Chapter 18: Case Studies in 3D Game Development

Understanding the theoretical aspects of 3D game development is essential, but seeing these concepts in action can provide invaluable insights. In this chapter, we will explore three detailed case studies that highlight different genres of 3D games: a simple first-person shooter (FPS), a puzzle adventure game, and a multiplayer racing game. Each case study will delve into the game's design, development process, challenges faced, and the solutions implemented. By examining these examples, aspiring game developers can gain a deeper appreciation for the nuances of 3D game development and learn practical strategies for their projects.

Case Study 1: Building a Simple First-Person Shooter

Overview

The first-person shooter genre has been one of the most popular and enduring in video game history. In this case study, we will look at the development of a simple FPS called "Pixel Warfare," designed to be an accessible entry point for both players and developers.

Game Concept

"Pixel Warfare" is a retro-style FPS that allows players to engage in fast-paced multiplayer combat in pixelated environments. The game features basic mechanics, such as shooting, jumping, and picking up power-ups.

Development Process

1. **Choosing the Right Tools**: The development team decided to use Three.js for rendering and Babylon.js for physics. These libraries provided the necessary tools to create a visually appealing game with robust physics without requiring extensive knowledge of WebGL.

2. **Setting Up the Project**: The team began by creating a project structure, including directories for assets, scripts, and styles. They set up a local server to facilitate easy testing and debugging.

3. **Creating the Game Environment**: The developers designed a simple arena using basic geometric shapes. They created walls, platforms, and obstacles to enhance gameplay. This environment was textured with pixel art to maintain the retro aesthetic.

4. **Implementing Player Controls**: The team programmed basic player controls using JavaScript. This included movement (WASD keys), jumping (spacebar), and shooting (mouse click). They ensured that the controls were responsive to provide a smooth gaming experience.

5. **Adding Enemies**: Basic AI was implemented to create enemy characters that patrolled the environment and attacked players upon detection. The AI behavior was simple but effective, adding an extra layer of challenge.

6. **Game Mechanics**: The core game mechanics were implemented, including health systems, weapon pickups, and score tracking. The team focused on balancing gameplay to ensure that it was engaging and challenging without being frustrating.

7. **Testing and Feedback**: After the initial development phase, the team conducted playtests to gather feedback. They observed players interacting with the game and took notes on areas for improvement.

This feedback loop was crucial for refining game mechanics and user experience.

Challenges Faced

- **Physics and Collisions**: One of the primary challenges was implementing accurate collision detection between players, bullets, and the environment. The team utilized Babylon.js's physics engine to handle collisions effectively.
- **Networking for Multiplayer**: Implementing a multiplayer mode posed a significant challenge. The team opted to use WebSockets for real-time communication. They developed a simple server that handled player connections and synchronized game states across clients.

Solutions Implemented

- **Physics Tuning**: To address the collision detection issues, the team spent time fine-tuning physics properties, such as friction and restitution. They also implemented a more granular collision detection system that accounted for different object types.
- **Optimizing Networking**: To minimize latency and ensure smooth gameplay, the team implemented client-side prediction for player movements. This technique allowed players to see their movements instantly while the server reconciled the final positions.

Results

"Pixel Warfare" successfully launched with positive feedback from players. The game's retro aesthetic, simple mechanics, and engaging multiplayer experience attracted a dedicated player base. The team learned valuable lessons about physics, networking, and the importance of player feedback in game development.

Case Study 2: Creating a Puzzle Adventure Game

Overview

Puzzle adventure games blend storytelling with challenging gameplay, offering players an immersive experience. In this case study, we will explore the development of "Mystic Quest," a 3D puzzle adventure game designed for players of all ages.

Game Concept

"Mystic Quest" takes players on a journey through a mystical world filled with puzzles, challenges, and rich storytelling. Players assume the role of a young adventurer who must solve puzzles to progress through various levels and uncover the secrets of the enchanted land.

Development Process

1. **Game Design Document**: The development team started with a comprehensive game design document (GDD) outlining the game's mechanics, story, characters, and levels. This document served as a roadmap throughout development.
2. **Choosing the Technology Stack**: The team chose Three.js for 3D rendering, along with the A-Frame framework for easy integration of 3D models and scene management. They utilized Tiled for level design, allowing them to create intricate and engaging puzzles.
3. **Creating the Game World**: The team designed diverse environments, including forests, caves, and castles. Each environment was populated with interactive objects, such as switches, levers, and doors, which players could manipulate to solve puzzles.
4. **Implementing Puzzle Mechanics**: The core of the game revolved around various puzzle mechanics, such as combination locks, environmental puzzles, and logic-based challenges. The team focused on

creating intuitive mechanics that encouraged players to think critically.

5. **Storytelling and Characters**: The game featured a rich narrative with memorable characters. The team wrote dialogue and implemented a branching dialogue system that allowed players to make choices that influenced the story's outcome.

6. **User Interface Design**: A clean and intuitive user interface was essential for guiding players through the game. The team created an inventory system to manage items collected throughout the adventure and implemented hints to assist players who may be struggling.

7. **Playtesting and Iteration**: The team conducted multiple rounds of playtesting to evaluate puzzle difficulty, pacing, and user experience. Feedback was gathered from testers to fine-tune puzzles and enhance the overall gameplay experience.

Challenges Faced

- **Puzzle Design**: One of the significant challenges was designing puzzles that were challenging yet solvable. The team had to strike a balance between complexity and accessibility to ensure players remained engaged.

- **Performance Optimization**: As the game world expanded, performance issues arose, particularly with rendering large environments. The team needed to optimize models and textures to maintain smooth performance across various devices.

Solutions Implemented

- **Iterative Puzzle Design**: To tackle puzzle design challenges, the team adopted an iterative approach. They created prototypes for each puzzle and tested them extensively, ensuring that players found them engaging without feeling overwhelmed.

- **Level of Detail (LOD) Techniques**: To optimize performance, the team implemented LOD techniques, reducing the complexity of 3D models based on the camera distance. This approach ensured that only the necessary details were rendered, enhancing performance without sacrificing visual quality.

Results

"Mystic Quest" received positive reviews for its captivating story, engaging puzzles, and immersive world. The team successfully created a game that appealed to a wide audience, showcasing the potential of 3D puzzle adventure games. The development process emphasized the importance of player feedback, puzzle iteration, and performance optimization.

Case Study 3: Developing a Multiplayer Racing Game

Overview

Racing games offer fast-paced action and competition, making them a popular choice among players. In this case study, we will examine the development of "Speed Racers," a multiplayer racing game designed to provide an exciting online racing experience.

Game Concept

"Speed Racers" features colorful and dynamic tracks set in vibrant environments. Players can choose from various vehicles, each with unique characteristics, and compete against others in real-time races.

Development Process

1. **Initial Concept and Design**: The development team outlined the game's concept, focusing on fun and competitive racing. They established core gameplay mechanics, including drifting, boosting, and track shortcuts.
2. **Choosing the Technology Stack**: The team opted for Three.js for

3D rendering and a custom Node.js server for handling multiplayer functionality. The decision to use WebSockets enabled real-time communication between players and the server.

3. **Track Design**: The team designed various race tracks, each with unique themes and challenges. They used a combination of Blender and Tiled for creating track layouts and assets, ensuring smooth transitions between sections.

4. **Vehicle Physics**: Implementing realistic vehicle physics was crucial for an engaging racing experience. The team used the Cannon.js physics engine to simulate vehicle movement, including acceleration, braking, and collisions.

5. **Multiplayer Functionality**: The team focused on creating a seamless multiplayer experience. They implemented player matchmaking, race lobbies, and real-time updates to ensure smooth synchronization of game states.

6. **User Interface Design**: A user-friendly interface was designed to allow players to select vehicles, view race results, and track their progress. The UI was integrated with the racing mechanics, providing real-time updates on lap times and positions.

7. **Testing and Balancing**: Extensive testing was conducted to balance vehicle performance and track design. The team organized multiplayer playtests to evaluate game dynamics, ensure fairness, and refine game-play mechanics.

Challenges Faced

- **Network Latency**: One of the significant challenges was managing network latency in multiplayer races. Players' actions needed to be synchronized in real-time to ensure a fair and enjoyable experience.
- **Balancing Vehicles**: Ensuring that all vehicles had unique characteristics without being overpowered was a challenge. The team had to balance speed, handling, and acceleration to create an engaging racing experience.

Solutions Implemented

- **Client-Side Prediction**: To address network latency, the team implemented client-side prediction for player movements. This allowed players to see their actions instantly while the server reconciled the final positions, minimizing the impact of lag.
- **Extensive Playtesting**: To balance vehicle performance, the team conducted extensive playtesting, gathering feedback on vehicle characteristics. They iteratively adjusted parameters until a satisfactory balance was achieved.

Results

"Speed Racers" became a hit among players, thanks to its engaging multiplayer experience, vibrant visuals, and competitive gameplay. The case study highlighted the importance of network optimization, vehicle balancing, and player feedback in creating successful racing games.

Through these case studies, we have explored the diverse approaches to 3D game development across different genres. Each case study emphasized the importance of thorough planning, effective use of technology, and continuous player feedback. Whether creating a simple FPS, a captivating puzzle adventure, or an exhilarating multiplayer racing game, the principles of design, development, and testing remain consistent. By learning from these examples, aspiring game developers can gain valuable insights to inform their projects and enhance their skills in the ever-evolving world of 3D game development.

Chapter 19: Expanding Your Skills

As you progress in your 3D game development journey, the desire to enhance your skills and broaden your horizons is natural. The landscape of game development is ever-evolving, with new tools, technologies, and techniques emerging regularly. In this chapter, we will explore various resources for further learning, delve into alternative game engines that offer JavaScript integration, discuss the importance of community involvement, and outline potential next steps to further your 3D game development career.

Resources for Further Learning

Online Courses and Tutorials

One of the best ways to expand your skills is through online courses and tutorials. Various platforms offer structured learning paths for 3D game development, covering everything from basics to advanced techniques. Here are some notable platforms:

- **Udemy**: Udemy offers a wide range of courses tailored to different skill levels. Look for courses focusing on Three.js, Babylon.js, WebGL, and game design principles. These courses often include hands-on projects that allow you to apply what you learn.
- **Coursera**: Collaborating with renowned universities, Coursera provides comprehensive courses on game design and development. Many of these

courses offer certification, adding value to your resume.

- **Pluralsight**: Known for its tech-focused courses, Pluralsight provides in-depth training on JavaScript, game engines, and 3D graphics. Their courses are often taught by industry experts, offering insights that are directly applicable to real-world projects.
- **YouTube**: YouTube hosts a wealth of tutorials and lectures covering specific aspects of 3D game development. Channels like "The Coding Train," "Three.js Fundamentals," and "Brackeys" (for Unity) offer high-quality, free content that can complement your learning.

Books and Documentation

Books remain a vital resource for deepening your understanding of 3D game development. Here are some recommended titles:

- **"Learning Three.js: The JavaScript 3D Library for WebGL" by Jos Dirksen**: This book provides a hands-on approach to learning Three.js, covering everything from basic concepts to advanced techniques.
- **"Game Programming Patterns" by Robert Nystrom**: This book explores common programming patterns in game development, offering insights into architecture and design that can improve your code quality.
- **"Real-Time Rendering" by Tomas Akenine-Möller et al.**: A comprehensive guide to rendering techniques, this book is suitable for developers interested in understanding the theory behind 3D graphics.
- **Documentation and API References**: Familiarize yourself with the official documentation for libraries and engines you use. The Three.js documentation is an invaluable resource, providing examples and explanations of various features. Similarly, explore the Babylon.js and WebGL documentation for deeper insights.

Online Communities and Forums

Engaging with online communities can provide support, inspiration, and opportunities to learn from others. Here are some popular platforms where you can connect with fellow developers:

- **Stack Overflow**: This question-and-answer site is an excellent resource for troubleshooting and seeking advice. You can ask questions related to specific coding issues or search for existing answers.
- **Reddit**: Subreddits like r/gamedev and r/3Dmodeling are vibrant communities where developers share experiences, showcase projects, and discuss industry trends. Participating in these discussions can offer new perspectives and insights.
- **Discord Servers**: Many game development communities have Discord servers where members can chat, share resources, and collaborate on projects. Look for servers dedicated to 3D game development, JavaScript, or specific engines like Three.js or Babylon.js.
- **GitHub**: Explore open-source projects on GitHub related to game development. Contributing to these projects can enhance your skills while allowing you to collaborate with other developers.

Exploring Other Game Engines: Unity and Unreal with JavaScript Integration

While this book primarily focuses on 3D game development with JavaScript using Three.js and Babylon.js, there are other powerful game engines worth exploring. Unity and Unreal Engine are two of the most widely used engines in the industry, both offering JavaScript integration in various forms.

Unity

Unity is a versatile game engine widely used for 2D and 3D game development. While C# is the primary programming language for Unity, you can integrate JavaScript (UnityScript) for specific tasks, though Unity has deprecated it. However, learning Unity is valuable as it allows developers to create cross-platform games with extensive community support and resources.

Key Features of Unity:

- **Asset Store**: Unity's Asset Store offers a vast collection of assets, tools, and plugins that can accelerate your development process. You can find everything from 3D models to pre-built game mechanics.
- **Visual Scripting**: Unity includes a visual scripting tool called Bolt, allowing developers to create gameplay mechanics without writing code. This feature is beneficial for artists and designers who may not be proficient in programming.
- **Multiplatform Support**: Unity enables developers to deploy their games across various platforms, including PC, consoles, mobile devices, and web browsers.
- **Robust Community and Resources**: Unity has a large and active community, making it easy to find tutorials, forums, and documentation to assist you in your development journey.

Unreal Engine

Unreal Engine is known for its high-quality graphics and is often used in AAA game development. Similar to Unity, Unreal primarily uses C++, but it also offers a visual scripting system called Blueprints, which allows developers to create gameplay elements without extensive programming knowledge.

Key Features of Unreal Engine:

- **High-Quality Graphics**: Unreal Engine excels in producing stunning visuals, making it a popular choice for developers aiming for realistic graphics in their games.

- **Blueprint Visual Scripting**: Blueprints enable developers to design game logic visually, making it accessible for non-programmers to contribute to game development.
- **Marketplace**: Unreal Engine's Marketplace offers various assets and plugins to enhance your game development process.
- **Cross-Platform Development**: Unreal Engine supports a wide range of platforms, allowing developers to reach diverse audiences.

Integrating JavaScript with Unity and Unreal

While Unity and Unreal Engine primarily use C# and C++ respectively, integrating JavaScript is still possible through various methods:

- **Unity**: Although UnityScript is deprecated, you can use JavaScript in WebGL builds through Unity's JavaScript Web APIs. This allows you to interact with web elements while maintaining the core game logic in C#.
- **Unreal Engine**: You can use JavaScript in Unreal Engine through plugins or by using Node.js for server-side applications. This integration allows for dynamic content delivery and enhances your game's functionality.

Joining the 3D Game Development Community

Involvement in the game development community can significantly enrich your learning experience and open doors for collaboration and networking. Here are some ways to engage with the community:

Attend Game Development Events

Participating in game development conferences, workshops, and meetups can provide invaluable networking opportunities and insights into industry trends. Some popular events include:

- **Game Developers Conference (GDC)**: GDC is one of the largest gatherings of game developers, featuring talks, panels, and networking opportunities.
- **PAX (Various Locations)**: PAX events offer opportunities to meet fellow developers, playtest games, and attend panels on various topics in game development.
- **Local Meetups**: Many cities have local game development meetups where developers can share their work, collaborate, and learn from one another.

Contribute to Open Source Projects

Contributing to open-source projects is a great way to enhance your skills while collaborating with others. Many game development libraries and tools are open source, and you can find repositories on platforms like GitHub.

Participate in Game Jams

Game jams are events where developers come together to create games within a short timeframe, usually 48 to 72 hours. Participating in game jams can help you hone your skills, collaborate with others, and create a portfolio of work. Some popular game jam platforms include:

- **Global Game Jam**: A worldwide event that encourages developers to create games based on a common theme.
- **Ludum Dare**: An online game jam that has been running for over a decade, offering a platform for developers to showcase their creativity.

Next Steps in Your 3D Game Development Journey

As you continue to develop your skills in 3D game development, consider the following steps to enhance your knowledge and experience:

Create Personal Projects

Start building your projects to apply what you've learned. Create small games or prototypes that incorporate various elements of 3D game development, such as mechanics, graphics, and sound. These projects can serve as valuable additions to your portfolio and demonstrate your capabilities to potential employers.

Collaborate with Others

Seek opportunities to collaborate with fellow developers, artists, and designers. Teaming up on projects can provide diverse perspectives and skills, enriching your development experience. Look for collaboration opportunities in online communities, game jams, or local meetups.

Explore Advanced Topics

As you become more comfortable with the fundamentals, consider exploring advanced topics in game development. Some areas to explore include:

- **Procedural Generation**: Learn how to create content algorithmically, allowing for dynamic and unique experiences in your games.
- **Artificial Intelligence**: Study AI techniques for creating intelligent NPC behavior and pathfinding systems.
- **Augmented and Virtual Reality**: Investigate how to develop immersive experiences using AR and VR technologies.

Stay Updated with Industry Trends

The game development industry is constantly evolving, so staying informed about the latest trends, tools, and technologies is essential. Follow industry blogs, podcasts, and news outlets to keep your knowledge current.

Consider Formal Education

If you're serious about a career in game development, consider pursuing formal education in game design, computer science, or a related field. Many universities and colleges offer specialized programs that can provide you with a solid foundation and valuable connections in the industry.

Build a Portfolio

As you complete projects and gain experience, create a portfolio showcasing your work. Include screenshots, gameplay videos, and descriptions of each project. A well-organized portfolio can be a powerful tool when applying for jobs or freelance opportunities.

Expanding your skills in 3D game development is a continuous journey filled with opportunities for growth and exploration. By leveraging online resources, engaging with the community, exploring alternative game engines, and pursuing personal projects, you can enhance your skills and prepare for a successful career in this exciting field. Remember that learning is an ongoing process, and every project you undertake brings you one step closer to mastering the art of 3D game development. Embrace the challenges, stay curious, and let your creativity guide you on this exhilarating journey.

Chapter 20: Final Project: Building a Complete 3D Game

In this chapter, we will embark on an exciting journey to build a complete 3D game using the skills and techniques you have acquired throughout this book. The final project will encapsulate all the concepts you've learned, providing a comprehensive overview of the 3D game development process. We'll start by defining our game idea, then set up the project structure, develop the core mechanics, add sound and effects, and finally, test and polish the game. By the end of this chapter, you will have a functional 3D game that you can share with others.

Defining the Game Idea

The first step in any game development process is defining your game idea. This involves conceptualizing the game's core mechanics, themes, and objectives. For this final project, we will create a simple 3D platformer game titled "**Space Explorer.**"

Game Concept

In "**Space Explorer,**" players will navigate a small spaceship through a series of increasingly difficult obstacles and challenges in space. The primary goal is to collect space crystals while avoiding asteroids and other hazards. The game will feature the following key elements:

181

- **Player Character**: A spaceship controlled by the player.
- **Obstacles**: Asteroids and other hazards that the player must avoid.
- **Collectibles**: Space crystals that the player collects for points.
- **Levels**: Multiple levels with increasing difficulty and different layouts.
- **Scoring System**: Points awarded for each crystal collected.

Game Mechanics

To create an engaging experience, we will incorporate several game mechanics, including:

- **Player Movement**: The player will control the spaceship using keyboard input for movement.
- **Collision Detection**: The game will detect collisions between the player's spaceship and obstacles, resulting in a game over.
- **Scoring System**: Players will earn points for each crystal collected, encouraging exploration.
- **Level Progression**: The game will consist of multiple levels, each with unique layouts and challenges.

Visual Style

The visual style of **"Space Explorer"** will feature a simple yet colorful aesthetic, with a starry background, vibrant obstacles, and glowing collectibles. The design will aim for a cartoonish look that appeals to a wide audience.

Setting Up the Project Structure

Once the game idea is defined, the next step is to set up the project structure. A well-organized project will help streamline the development process and make it easier to manage assets and code.

Creating the Project Directory

1. **Project Root Folder**: Create a new folder named SpaceExplorer on your computer. This will serve as the root directory for your project.
2. **Subfolders**: Inside the SpaceExplorer folder, create the following subfolders:

- src: For all source code files (JavaScript).
- assets: For all game assets, including models, textures, and sounds.
- css: For stylesheets.
- index.html: The main HTML file to launch the game.
- README.md: A file to document the project structure, installation instructions, and gameplay details.

Basic HTML Structure

Create the index.html file in the root directory and set up a basic HTML structure:

```html
Copy code
<!DOCTYPE html>
<html lang="en">
<head>
    <meta charset="UTF-8">
    <meta name="viewport" content="width=device-width,
    initial-scale=1.0">
    <title>Space Explorer</title>
    <link rel="stylesheet" href="css/styles.css">
    <script
    src="https://cdnjs.cloudflare.com/ajax/libs/three.js/r128/three.
    min.js"></script> <script src="src/main.js" defer></script>
</head>
<body>
    <h1>Welcome to Space Explorer!</h1>
```

```
    <div id="game-container"></div>
  </body>
  </html>
```

Setting Up the CSS

Create a basic styles.css file in the css folder to style your game container:

```css
Copy code
body {
    margin: 0;
    display: flex;
    flex-direction: column;
    align-items: center;
    background-color: #000;
    color: #fff;
}

#game-container {
    width: 100vw;
    height: 100vh;
    overflow: hidden;
}
```

Developing the Core Game Mechanics

With the project structure in place, we can now focus on developing the core game mechanics. This involves setting up the Three.js scene, adding the player spaceship, implementing movement, and handling collisions.

Creating the Game Scene

Open the main.js file in the src folder and begin by setting up the Three.js scene, camera, and renderer:

```javascript
Copy code
// src/main.js

// Import necessary modules
import * as THREE from 'three';

// Create the scene
const scene = new THREE.Scene();
const camera = new THREE.PerspectiveCamera(75, window.innerWidth /
window.innerHeight, 0.1, 1000);
const renderer = new THREE.WebGLRenderer({ antialias: true });
renderer.setSize(window.innerWidth, window.innerHeight); document.
getElementById('game-container').appendChild

(renderer.domElement);

// Set the camera position
camera.position.z = 5;

// Create a basic animation loop
const animate = function () {
    requestAnimationFrame(animate);
    renderer.render(scene, camera);
};

// Start the animation
animate();
```

Adding the Player Spaceship

Next, let's add the player spaceship to the scene. We will create a simple geometry to represent the spaceship.

```javascript
Copy code
// Create the spaceship
const spaceshipGeometry = new THREE.ConeGeometry(0.5, 1, 8);
const spaceshipMaterial = new THREE.MeshBasicMaterial({ color:
0xff0000 });
const spaceship = new THREE.Mesh(spaceshipGeometry,
spaceshipMaterial);
scene.add(spaceship);
```

Implementing Player Movement

To control the spaceship, we'll use keyboard input. Add event listeners for key presses to move the spaceship left and right.

```javascript
Copy code
let moveSpeed = 0.1;
let spaceshipDirection = 0;

document.addEventListener('keydown', (event) => {
    if (event.code === 'ArrowLeft') {
        spaceshipDirection = -1;
    } else if (event.code === 'ArrowRight') {
        spaceshipDirection = 1;
    }
});

document.addEventListener('keyup', (event) => {
    if (event.code === 'ArrowLeft' || event.code === 'ArrowRight')
    {
        spaceshipDirection = 0;
    }
});

// Update spaceship position in the animation loop
```

```
const animate = function () {
    requestAnimationFrame(animate);
    spaceship.rotation.y += spaceshipDirection * moveSpeed;
    renderer.render(scene, camera);
};

animate();
```

Adding Obstacles

Next, let's add obstacles for the player to avoid. We'll create a few simple geometries that will act as asteroids.

```
javascript
Copy code
function createAsteroid() {
    const asteroidGeometry = new THREE.SphereGeometry(0.5, 8, 8);
    const asteroidMaterial = new THREE.MeshBasicMaterial({ color:
    0x808080 });
    const asteroid = new THREE.Mesh(asteroidGeometry,
    asteroidMaterial);

    asteroid.position.x = (Math.random() - 0.5) * 10;
    asteroid.position.y = (Math.random() - 0.5) * 10;
    asteroid.position.z = Math.random() * -20 - 5;

    scene.add(asteroid);
}

// Create multiple asteroids
for (let i = 0; i < 10; i++) {
    createAsteroid();
}
```

Collision Detection

To ensure the player can lose the game by hitting an obstacle, we need to implement collision detection. This can be achieved by checking the distance between the spaceship and each asteroid.

```javascript
Copy code
function checkCollisions() {
    scene.children.forEach((child) => {
        if (child !== spaceship && child.type === 'Mesh') {
            const distance =
            spaceship.position.distanceTo(child.position);
            if (distance < 1) {
                // Handle collision (e.g., reset game, show game
                over)
                console.log('Collision detected!');
                // You may want to stop the game or reset
                positions here
            }
        }
    });
}
```

Updating the Animation Loop

Finally, update the animation loop to include collision checks:

```javascript
Copy code
const animate = function () {
    requestAnimationFrame(animate);
    spaceship.rotation.y += spaceshipDirection * moveSpeed;
    checkCollisions();
    renderer.render(scene, camera);
```

```
};

animate();
```

Adding Sound, Effects, and Polishing

With the core game mechanics in place, it's time to enhance the game with sound effects, visual effects, and other polish. These elements will significantly improve the player experience.

Adding Sound Effects

Using the Web Audio API, we can add sound effects for collecting crystals and detecting collisions.

Loading Sound Files

First, create a folder in the assets directory called sounds, and add your sound files (e.g., collect.mp3, collision.mp3). Next, implement sound loading in your main.js:

```javascript
Copy code
// Load sound files
const audioLoader = new THREE.AudioLoader();
const collectSound = new THREE.Audio(new THREE.AudioListener());
const collisionSound = new THREE.Audio(new THREE.AudioListener());

audioLoader.load('assets/sounds/collect.mp3', (buffer) => {
    collectSound.setBuffer(buffer);
    collectSound.setVolume(0.5);
});

audioLoader.load('assets/sounds/collision.mp3', (buffer) => {
    collisionSound.setBuffer(buffer);
    collisionSound.setVolume(0.5);
```

```
});
```

Playing Sound Effects

Next, trigger sound effects at appropriate events in the game, such as collecting crystals or colliding with obstacles.

```javascript
javascript
Copy code
function collectCrystal() {
    collectSound.play();
    // Additional logic for collecting crystals (e.g., updating
    score)
}

function checkCollisions() {
    scene.children.forEach((child) => {
        if (child !== spaceship && child.type === 'Mesh') {
            const distance =
            spaceship.position.distanceTo(child.position);
            if (distance < 1) {
                collisionSound.play();
                // Handle collision (e.g., reset game, show game
                over)
                console.log('Collision detected!');
            }
        }
    });
}
```

Adding Visual Effects

In addition to sound, visual effects can enhance the game's atmosphere. Consider adding particle effects for collecting items or explosions when colliding.

Implementing Particle Effects

Create a simple particle system using Three.js. You can use sprites or a geometry-based approach to create visual effects when collecting items.

```javascript
Copy code
function createParticleEffect(position) {
    const particles = new THREE.Geometry();

    for (let i = 0; i < 100; i++) {
        const vertex = new THREE.Vector3();
        vertex.x = position.x + (Math.random() - 0.5);
        vertex.y = position.y + (Math.random() - 0.5);
        vertex.z = position.z + (Math.random() - 0.5);
        particles.vertices.push(vertex);
    }

    const particleMaterial = new THREE.PointsMaterial({ color:
    0xff0000, size: 0.1 });
    const particleSystem = new THREE.Points(particles,
    particleMaterial);
    scene.add(particleSystem);

    // Add logic to remove the particle effect after a short
    duration
}
```

Polishing the Game

Lastly, take some time to polish the game. This includes refining the user interface (UI), adding a main menu, and providing clear instructions for gameplay. Consider adding a score display to show the player's current score and how many crystals they have collected.

```javascript
Copy code
// Example of adding a score display
let score = 0;
```

```
function updateScoreDisplay() {
    const scoreElement = document.createElement('div');
    scoreElement.style.position = 'absolute';
    scoreElement.style.color = '#fff';
    scoreElement.style.top = '10px';
    scoreElement.style.left = '10px';
    scoreElement.innerText = `Score: ${score}`;
    document.body.appendChild(scoreElement);
}

function collectCrystal() {
    collectSound.play();
    score++;
    updateScoreDisplay();
}
```

Testing and Final Touches

After implementing sound effects and visual polish, the final step is to test the game thoroughly and make any necessary adjustments.

Playtesting

Playtest your game multiple times to identify any issues, bugs, or areas for improvement. Ask friends or fellow developers to play the game and provide feedback. Consider aspects such as:

- **Difficulty**: Is the game too easy or too hard?
- **Controls**: Are the controls responsive and intuitive?
- **Fun Factor**: Is the game enjoyable to play?

Bug Fixes

Address any bugs or glitches that arise during testing. Common issues might include:

- Collision detection problems.
- Performance issues when rendering too many objects.
- Sound not playing as expected.

Final Touches

Make final adjustments based on feedback and testing results. This might involve tweaking gameplay mechanics, adjusting the user interface, or enhancing visual effects. Ensure that your game is polished and ready for others to enjoy.

Congratulations! You have successfully built a complete 3D game titled **"Space Explorer."** This project encapsulates the essential aspects of 3D game development, from conceptualizing the game idea to implementing mechanics, sound effects, and visual polish. Remember that game development is an iterative process, and there is always room for improvement and expansion. Use this project as a foundation to explore more complex ideas, incorporate additional features, and continue your journey in 3D game development. Embrace creativity, keep learning, and have fun creating new experiences for players around the world!

Final Conclusion: Mastering 3D Game Development with JavaScript

As we reach the conclusion of our journey through **"Mastering 3D Game Development with JavaScript,"** it's essential to reflect on the comprehensive landscape of skills, concepts, and practical applications you have explored in this book. Game development is an ever-evolving field that requires a blend of creativity, technical know-how, and problem-solving abilities. Whether you're a novice looking to create your first game or a seasoned developer seeking to refine your craft, this book has equipped you with the knowledge and tools to thrive in the exciting world of 3D game development.

Reflecting on the Journey

Throughout the chapters, we have laid a solid foundation for understanding the principles of 3D game development. From the basics of setting up a game environment using Three.js to implementing advanced features like physics engines, character animations, sound design, and multiplayer capabilities, each section has built upon the last, providing a cohesive learning experience.

Building Blocks of Game Development

We began our journey by exploring the core building blocks of game development. In the early chapters, we discussed setting up the Three.js library, creating 3D scenes, and understanding the fundamental components such as cameras, lights, and geometries. You learned how to manipulate objects in a virtual space, giving you the tools to create engaging environments. These initial lessons are crucial, as they form the backbone of any successful game.

Understanding the Role of Game Engines

A significant aspect of our exploration was understanding how game engines like Three.js operate. We delved into the advantages of using a framework for game development, which allows for rapid prototyping and experimentation. The concepts of rendering, animations, and materials became second nature as we dissected the components of Three.js. This foundational knowledge is invaluable, as it enables you to build games that are not only visually appealing but also performant.

Expanding Your Skill Set

As we progressed through the book, we shifted our focus toward more complex topics such as physics integration, character design, and AI implementation. These chapters challenged you to think critically about game mechanics and player interactions. By introducing physics engines like Cannon.js and Ammo.js, you learned how to simulate realistic movements and interactions within your game world. This knowledge is pivotal for creating immersive experiences that resonate with players.

Creating Engaging Characters and NPCs

Designing and animating player characters, along with implementing non-player characters (NPCs), added depth to your game development skill set. Understanding basic AI principles, movement patterns, and behavior trees empowers you to create more dynamic and interactive worlds. The ability to craft meaningful interactions through dialogue and quest systems enhances the player's engagement, making your games more enjoyable and replayable.

The Importance of Visual and Auditory Elements

A significant aspect of game development is creating an atmosphere that captivates players. Through the exploration of materials and shaders, you learned how to enhance the visual quality of your games. By understanding the principles of lighting, shading, and texturing, you can create stunning visual effects that elevate the player experience.

Similarly, the integration of sound design and music plays a crucial role in crafting immersive environments. The chapters on working with sound and music emphasized the importance of auditory feedback in gameplay. From background music to sound effects triggered by events, audio elements can significantly influence player emotions and responses, making your game world feel more alive and engaging.

Performance Optimization and Debugging

As any seasoned developer knows, creating a game is only half the battle. Optimizing performance is essential for ensuring a smooth and enjoyable gaming experience. In the chapters dedicated to performance optimization, you explored various techniques to reduce model complexity, implement level of detail (LOD) strategies, and manage memory effectively. These skills are vital for ensuring that your games run smoothly across various devices and platforms.

Moreover, we delved into debugging and testing, highlighting the importance of identifying and resolving issues early in the development process. The tools and methodologies discussed enable you to refine your code, ensuring that your games are both functional and enjoyable.

Engaging with Multiplayer Development

As gaming evolves, so too does the expectation for multiplayer experiences. The chapters dedicated to multiplayer game development introduced you to concepts like WebSockets and game state synchronization. Understanding how to handle latency and lag compensation equips you with the skills to create real-time multiplayer experiences that keep players engaged and connected.

Final Project: Synthesis of Knowledge

The culmination of your learning journey was the final project, where you built a complete 3D game titled **"Space Explorer."** This hands-on experience synthesized all the concepts you learned throughout the book. By defining a game idea, developing core mechanics, adding sound and effects, and polishing your game, you demonstrated your ability to apply your knowledge practically. This project not only serves as a testament to your skills but also as a foundation for future projects.

Looking Ahead: The Future of Game Development

As you close this book and reflect on your journey through 3D game development with JavaScript, it's essential to look ahead and consider the vast opportunities that lie before you. The gaming industry is continuously evolving, driven by technological advancements, changing player preferences, and new creative possibilities.

Continuous Learning and Adaptation

The key to thriving in this dynamic field is to remain curious and committed to continuous learning. The concepts you've mastered in this book are just the beginning. As new tools, frameworks, and techniques emerge, staying updated will empower you to push the boundaries of your creativity.

Exploring New Game Engines

While you've gained proficiency in Three.js, consider exploring other game engines such as Unity and Unreal Engine. Each engine has its strengths, and learning to work with different tools broadens your skill set and opens new avenues for creativity. Unity, for instance, provides a rich ecosystem for 2D and 3D game development, while Unreal Engine offers advanced rendering capabilities and is widely used in the industry.

Joining the Game Development Community

Engaging with the game development community is an invaluable way to share knowledge, receive feedback, and stay inspired. Participate in online forums, attend local meetups, or join game development groups on social media. Collaboration and networking with fellow developers can lead to exciting opportunities and creative partnerships. Additionally, consider participating in game jams, where you can challenge yourself to create a game in a limited timeframe, fostering innovation and skill development.

Expanding Your Game Development Skills

Beyond technical skills, consider exploring aspects like game design, storytelling, and user experience. Understanding how to create compelling narratives and engaging gameplay loops enhances your ability to craft memorable experiences. Additionally, delving into topics like marketing and monetization will help you navigate the business side of game development, ensuring that your creations reach a wider audience.

The Joy of Creation

Game development is ultimately about creation and expression. The skills you've acquired in this book empower you to bring your ideas to life, share stories, and create experiences that resonate with players. Embrace your creativity and experiment with different genres, mechanics, and visual styles.

The beauty of game development lies in its potential for innovation and the ability to transport players to new worlds.

Final Thoughts

As you conclude this journey through **"Mastering 3D Game Development with JavaScript,"** take a moment to celebrate your accomplishments. You have built a solid foundation in game development, equipped with the knowledge and tools to create engaging and immersive 3D experiences. Remember that the path of a game developer is a continuous adventure, filled with challenges and triumphs. Embrace each experience, learn from your mistakes, and never stop pushing the boundaries of your creativity.

In closing, I encourage you to dive into your next project with enthusiasm and determination. Whether you choose to create a small indie game or embark on a more ambitious endeavor, trust in your skills and the knowledge you've gained. The gaming world is waiting for your unique voice and vision. Happy game developing!